Digital Factics: X

The Success Guide to Mastering Business Growth on X

Second Edition 2026

***

Basil C. Puglisi, MPA

A Human & AI Collaboration

Claude, Grok, Perplexity, Gemini,

ChatGPT, Le Chat, DeepSeek

used with HAIA-RECCLIN

* * *

Content, Strategy & Frameworks:

basilpuglisi.com

CONTENTS

1	Introduction to X	1
2	Setting Up Your Professional X Profile	18
3	Understanding X Premium & Verification	30
4	Content Strategy and Planning	40
5	Writing Posts & Threads That Perform	50
6	Using Multimedia on X	59
7	Scheduling, Tools, & Workflow	67
8	Understanding the X Algorithm	75
9	Hashtags, Tags, & Visibility Tactics	84
10	Collaborations & Cross-Promotion	91
11	Organic Growth Tactics	100
12	Content Planning for Consistency	108
13	Metrics & Analytics That Drive Decisions	116

14	**Monetizing Your X Efforts**	**126**
15	**Challenges and Risks on X**	**135**
16	**X Ads & Promoted Posts**	**144**
17	**Using AI & Automation Tools**	**153**
18	**Putting It All Together**	**160**

How This Book Works:

The Factics Method

This framework turns analysis into measurable outcomes through three elements appearing in every chapter.

Facts establish what exists through data and evidence. These are the research findings, platform statistics, and documented patterns that reveal how X actually works rather than how we assume it works.

Tactics define what to do through strategic action. These are the specific, repeatable steps you can implement based on the facts. Tactics without facts become guesswork. Facts without tactics become trivia.

Outcomes determine whether actions worked through measurable results. These are the specific goals you can track to verify progress. Without defined outcomes, you can't distinguish successful tactics from wasted effort.

The methodology reflects over two decades of refinement across social media strategy, enterprise transformation, and governance development. The structure maintains consistency whether analyzing profile optimization or content strategy driving faster follower growth.

Content without this structure becomes entertainment instead of value delivery. Strategy lacking actionable tactics generates awareness without capability. Recommendations lacking measurable outcomes prevent you from verifying success or failure.

The approach serves specific purpose addressing the gap where social media efforts fail. Many businesses can't measure current performance, can't implement systematic strategy, and can't assign accountability when results disappoint. This framework addresses each gap directly. Facts enable measurement. Tactics enable implementation. Outcomes create accountability.

The pattern repeats deliberately throughout the analysis. Research establishes baseline conditions. Platform dynamics explain why problems persist despite obvious solutions. Tactics provide responses appropriate to different business contexts and resource levels. Outcomes define success thresholds enabling you to measure progress rather than hoping for improvement.

This repetition proves intentional. Strategy requires muscle memory built through systematic practice. When every chapter shows the same structure, you internalize the approach enabling application beyond the specific examples examined here. The goal becomes not memorizing this analysis but mastering the methodology enabling your own strategic implementation across any platform or business challenge you encounter.

Content and Knowledge Disclaimer

All information in this book draws from publicly available sources, platform documentation, industry research, and the author's professional experience. Original sources receive proper attribution to validate claims and acknowledge shared ideas.

This book combines evidence-based platform analysis with proprietary methodologies (Factics and HAIA-RECCLIN) to present systematic, measurable, and ethically grounded X strategy. All AI-assisted research underwent verification through multiple AI models and author review for accuracy, integrity, and ethical alignment.

Because X's tools, policies, and algorithm behavior continue evolving rapidly, readers should confirm current requirements through authoritative sources including official X documentation at help.x.com, the X Developer Platform, and X Business resources at business.x.com.

This book references various social media platforms, scheduling tools, analytics services, and technology companies for research, analysis, and illustrative purposes only. Mention of any specific platform, company, product, or service doesn't constitute an endorsement, recommendation, or partnership.

All trademarks, service marks, and company names mentioned herein are the property of their respective owners. References to X, Twitter, Buffer, Hootsuite, Sprout Social, Canva, and other tools and organizations appear solely for factual documentation and practical guidance within the context of social media strategy.

The author maintains no business relationships, partnerships, sponsorships, or affiliations with any platform providers or technology companies discussed in this work. All analysis, conclusions, and recommendations represent independent research and professional judgment.

Case studies throughout this book represent composite examples synthesizing patterns from similar professional engagements. Metrics reflect documented ranges from actual implementations. Individual results vary based on execution quality, market conditions, audience characteristics, and competitive dynamics. The frameworks presented here represent operational approaches tested through documented practice. Readers should adapt strategies to their specific contexts, resources, and business requirements rather than implementing recommendations without contextual evaluation.

A Note on Platform Data

Platform specifications, pricing, and policies change frequently. The data in this book reflects X as of late 2025. Subscription tiers, monetization thresholds, and feature availability may have shifted since publication. For current information, verify details at X's official help center and business resources.

The strategic frameworks and methodology remain stable regardless of platform changes. When specific numbers shift, apply the same analytical approach to current data.

Third Party Brands, Trademarks, and No Endorsement Disclosure

This publication references third party companies, platforms, products, and services, including artificial intelligence platforms, social platforms, and software tools. All third party names, logos, product names, and trademarks are the property of their respective owners. Any use of these names or marks is for identification, commentary, editorial, or educational purposes only.

No Partnership, Sponsorship, or Endorsement

This publication is not affiliated with, sponsored by, endorsed by, or partnered with any third party company referenced. No third party company reviews, approves, or validates this publication. References to any third party platform or brand reflect the author's independent experience, observations, research, and applied use. Any performance outcomes described are context dependent and vary by audience, content, timing, budget, and platform changes.

Use of Logos, Icons, and Brand Assets

If third party logos, icons, or brand assets appear in this publication, they are used solely to identify the referenced platforms and to support educational and explanatory content. Such use does not imply endorsement or a commercial relationship. Brand assets are used in a manner intended to comply with applicable trademark and brand usage guidelines. If any third party rights holder believes an asset is used improperly, contact the publisher to request review and correction in future editions.

Screenshots, Interfaces, and Post Examples

Any screenshots, interface depictions, post renderings, or example layouts are included for illustrative and educational purposes. Where real posts are shown, they are presented as displayed on the relevant platform at the time of capture. Platform features, policies, names, pricing, and eligibility criteria change frequently, and examples may not reflect the current user experience.

Results, Metrics, and Demonstrations

Any metrics, outcomes, workflows, prompts, or demonstrations described are provided as examples of process and method. They are not a guarantee of results. Business outcomes depend on many variables outside the author's control, including market conditions, creative quality, compliance decisions, audience fit, and platform algorithm changes.

AI Output and Human Responsibility Notice

This publication discusses the use of AI systems and may include AI assisted workflows, prompts, or examples. AI generated or AI assisted outputs can contain errors, omissions, outdated information, or unintended bias. The reader remains responsible for verification, compliance, and final decisions. Nothing in this publication constitutes professional legal, financial, medical, or regulatory advice.

Contact and Corrections

For corrections, rights concerns, or trademark related questions, contact the publisher or author at: digitalethos.org or author me@basilpuglisi.com.

About the Author

Basil C. Puglisi, MPA is a Human-AI Collaboration Strategist and Content Marketing Consultant whose work bridges over two decades of digital strategy evolution with advanced governance framework development.

His career spans the full arc of platform transformation, from early Web 2.0 community building through contemporary AI-enhanced enterprise workflows. This unique perspective informs the practical guidance throughout this book, connecting grassroots community wisdom with systematic modern methodology.

The journey started with Sweet Sounds Productions in 2002, promoted through AOL Instant Messenger and MySpace before most marketers understood social media. By the time the mobile and social revolutions arrived, he had already spent years studying how digital platforms reshape communication, commerce, and community.

In the late 2000s he founded DBMEi, known as Digital Brand Marketing Education and Interactives, which grew from a personal blog into Digital Ethos, a collaborative thought leadership platform with more than fifty contributors from academia, marketing, and technology. The community welcomed participation from organizations such as Google, NASA, and Microsoft, and gained recognition at major industry events including Social Media Week, SXSW, and SBA Weekends.

His most defining contribution came through Social Media Action Camps, gatherings built on a philosophy that remains powerful today: Teachers, not Speakers. Attendees did not leave merely inspired; they left equipped with templates, frameworks, and strategies ready to implement. Long before artificial intelligence would describe this as a legacy concept ahead of its time, Basil was already creating spaces centered on access, implementation, and empowerment.

Basil created two foundational methodologies shaping this work. The Factics Methodology (Facts + Tactics + Outcomes) provides systematic structure replacing aspirational advice with measurable accountability. The HAIA-RECCLIN Framework establishes seven specialized oversight roles (Researcher, Editor, Coder, Calculator, Liaison, Ideator, Navigator) ensuring human judgment remains sovereign over AI assistance.

In 2012 he published the first Digital Factics book, a 60-page MagCloud edition focused on Twitter strategy. Distributed at Social Media Week NYC, NY Expo, SXSW, and SBA events, it presented a simple but lasting idea: every fact connects to a tactic, and every tactic connects to a measurable outcome. Over a decade later, as Twitter evolved into X, that principle has never been more relevant.

He has authored more than one thousand articles on digital marketing and content strategy. His enterprise consulting focuses on AI transformation frameworks that preserve human decision authority through checkpoint-based governance protocols. Most importantly, he continues to build, test, and refine these systems through operational practice rather than theoretical speculation.

Acknowledgments

This work exists because of extraordinary collaborators who shared the vision that strategy requires systematic practice, not aspirational advice.

To the Digital Ethos and Social Media Action Camp teams, including Joy Lynskey, Craig Yaris, Bill Corbett Jr., Jeff Ogden, Louis Caparros DiCarlo, and Alison Gilbert: your commitment built not only projects but a movement.

To the communities at Digital Ethos and Social Media Club Long Island: thank you for proving that collaboration and generosity create greater value than competition ever could. Your commitment to collaborative knowledge building over competitive gatekeeping validated the distributed authority principles underlying this work.

To Chris Heuer and Kristie Wells: thank you for the Social Media Club International Board appointment at SXSW 2013. That opportunity showed how grassroots frameworks can achieve institutional recognition through operational validation rather than credentialing alone.

To my family: your support and patience are the foundation of everything I have built. You understood why systematic methodology development requires patience, iteration, and commitment to building capacity before opportunities arrive. You're the reason I stepped back into the light to complete what I began. To my sons: your morning hugs from behind me and evening chats watching me develop content, frameworks, and more was the inspiration and support needed to make unfinished projects become reality.

Let us begin again, armed with Factics.

Quick Start Guide:

Your First 24 Hours

If you have limited time today and want immediate progress, complete these three actions before reading further.

Action 1: Fix Your Bio (10 minutes)

Open your X profile and rewrite your bio using this formula: what you do, plus who you serve, plus one proof point. Example: "Marketing consultant helping B2B SaaS companies grow. 200+ clients served." Remove vague language like "passionate about" or "lover of." Add your location if you serve local clients.

Action 2: Pin Your Best Post (5 minutes)

Find your highest-performing post from the past 90 days. If you have no posts yet, write one introducing yourself and what value you provide. Pin it to the top of your profile. This is the first thing visitors see after your bio.

Action 3: Engage With Five People (15 minutes)

Find five posts in your industry from accounts with 1,000 to 50,000 followers. Add thoughtful replies that demonstrate your expertise. Not "Great post!" but actual substance that adds value to the conversation. This puts you in front of their audiences and signals to the algorithm that you're an active participant.

These three actions take 30 minutes total. They position your profile to convert visitors into followers and begin building relationships that compound over time. Now continue reading for the complete strategy.

Choose Your Path

Start Here:

This book serves readers at different stages of their X journey. Choose the path that matches your situation and available time.

Path 1: Small Business Owner (Limited Time)

Start with Quick Start Guide, then Chapter 2 (Profile Setup), Chapter 5 (Writing Posts), and Chapter 7 (Scheduling). Return to other chapters as your presence grows.

Path 2: Student or Career Learner (Building Foundation)

Read Chapters 1 through 6 sequentially to build foundational understanding. Focus on Chapter 4 (Content Strategy) and Chapter 8 (Algorithm) for competitive advantage in job markets.

Path 3: Marketing Practitioner (Advancing Skills)

Skip to Chapters 8 (Algorithm), 13 (Analytics), 14 (Monetization), and 16 (Advertising). These chapters provide advanced tactics for practitioners already comfortable with platform basics.

| 1 |

Introduction to X

Inside This Chapter

We examine who actually uses X and whether your customers are among them. The analysis establishes platform demographics, content velocity patterns, and strategic fit criteria. It documents the five business models where X excels and the situations where your time is better spent elsewhere. The chapter reveals baseline performance metrics for different account stages and a framework for deciding platform priority within your broader marketing strategy.

You open X and see posts moving at lightning speed. Breaking news, product launches, industry debates, customer complaints resolved publicly. Every minute brings new voices, new conversations, new opportunities. The question isn't whether X matters for your business but how to handle its velocity without burning out or getting lost in the noise.

This chapter answers that question with data backed positioning frameworks. You will learn where X fits in your social media strategy, which metrics matter for your specific goals, and how to make confident decisions about platform investment.

The Platform Overview in 2026

X, formerly Twitter, remains a significant platform despite ongoing changes. As of late 2025, the platform serves approximately 550 to 610 million monthly active users globally with approximately 245 million daily active users (DemandSage, 2025; Exploding Topics, 2025), positioning it as a major channel for 2026 business strategy. X doesn't publish official user counts, so figures represent industry estimates from analytics providers. Daily active users range from 130 million through app based usage to 250 million monetizable users depending on measurement methodology. This variance matters because different metrics measure different behaviors. App based users represent mobile engagement, while monetizable users include web traffic and represent advertising reach.

The United States, Japan, and India represent the largest user bases, though specific country-level figures vary by measurement methodology. Geographic distribution affects timing and cultural context. This geographic concentration creates targeting opportunities. If your business serves English speaking markets, Japanese consumers, or South Asian demographics, X provides concentrated access to these audiences.

Platform demographics reveal strategic opportunities worth understanding before investing your time. Users aged 25 to 34 comprise the largest segment at roughly 37 percent, while the 35 to 44 age bracket represents the highest engagement demographic. Gender distribution skews male at approximately 64 percent versus female at 36 percent.

These demographics matter when evaluating platform fit. If your target demographic skews male, ages 25 to 49, and professional or technology focused, X deserves priority consideration. B2B services, technology products, financial services, and professional development offerings align naturally with this user base. Consumer products targeting women under 25 may find better fit on Instagram or TikTok. The strategy here is straightforward: document your target customer demographics and calculate overlap with X's user base. If overlap exceeds 40 percent, X warrants weekly content investment. Track profile visits and follower growth weekly to confirm your audience actually shows up where the data suggests they should.

Content velocity on X exceeds other platforms significantly, with users generating hundreds of millions of posts daily in a high volume, real time ecosystem. This velocity shapes how you must approach the platform. Plan for higher posting frequency on X compared to Instagram or LinkedIn. Aim for minimum 5 to 7 posts weekly to maintain visibility in high velocity feeds. Track your weekly post count and monitor impressions per post. For accounts under 1,000 followers, target 500 to 2,000 impressions. If impressions drop below 300 consistently, increase posting frequency.

Video content drives significantly higher engagement than static text posts, with the algorithm prioritizing media that generates dwell time where users stop scrolling. Visual content including images and video consistently outperforms text-only posts in reach and engagement. These engagement patterns shape content strategy decisions. Incorporate video, even simple screen recordings or talking head clips, into roughly 30 percent of posts to use this engagement advantage.

Five Ways Businesses Win on X

Not every business needs every platform. Strategic platform selection requires matching platform strengths to business needs and resource capacity. X excels in five specific use cases. Understanding these helps you position the platform correctly within your broader marketing strategy.

Real time communication is where X dominates. Breaking news, live event coverage, crisis response, and time sensitive announcements perform better on X than any other platform. The feed structure prioritizes recency, making it ideal for communications where timing creates value. News organizations, event companies, political campaigns, sports teams, emergency services, and any business leveraging timely information as competitive advantage will find X essential.

Thought leadership rewards substantive ideas over aesthetic presentation. X's text forward format favors analysis over pretty pictures. Threads enable longer form thinking without requiring separate blog infrastructure. Industry experts, consultants, and executives use X to establish authority through insights and analysis. Professional services, consulting firms, B2B technology companies, industry analysts, executive personal brands, and businesses competing on expertise rather than product features find X particularly effective.

Community building happens through direct conversation. X enables dialogue with niche communities through replies, quote posts, and topic participation. Unlike LinkedIn's formal networking or Instagram's visual focus, X rewards authentic dialogue and consistent presence in relevant discussions. Creator economy businesses, membership communities, niche product companies, advocacy organizations, and brands building movements rather than just customer bases thrive here.

Customer service benefits from public visibility. Many customers prefer X for support because public visibility motivates faster response. Brands resolving issues publicly also build trust with observing audiences. Technology companies, consumer services, hospitality businesses, telecommunications providers, and any company where service quality differentiates from competitors can use this dynamic.

Content distribution uses X as amplification layer for owned media properties. Blog posts, podcasts, YouTube videos, newsletters, and long form content get amplified through X sharing. The platform's link friendly format makes it superior to Instagram for driving traffic to owned properties. Content creators, publishers, educators, course creators, SaaS companies with knowledge bases, and businesses using content marketing for lead generation find X effective for distribution.

Positioning X in Your Strategy

Strategic positioning requires matching X strengths to your business priorities. Start by identifying your primary social media goal. Choose one that drives platform prioritization: awareness, authority, traffic, community, or conversion. Document your primary goal because this determines how you evaluate platform fit and success metrics.

For awareness goals, X offers moderate potential. Viral posts reach massive audiences, but virality is unpredictable. Consistent posting with strategic engagement builds steady awareness growth. X works well for awareness if your target audience actively uses the platform.

For authority goals, X excels because threads enable showcasing expertise. Engagement with industry conversations positions you as active community participant. If authority drives your strategy, X deserves top priority.

For traffic goals, X performs well since link posts work naturally in X format. Users expect and click links more readily than on Instagram. If traffic generation matters, X should receive significant investment.

For community goals, X enables strong relationship building through direct replies that create conversations. Quote posts enable commentary that builds visibility. Participating in existing conversations builds relationships faster than broadcasting.

For conversion goals, X offers moderate fit. Direct selling often underperforms LinkedIn or email for B2B. However, X drives traffic to landing pages where conversion happens. Track click through rates on link posts to assess conversion pathway effectiveness.

Then assess your resource capacity honestly. X requires 30 to 60 minutes daily for effective management, including 20 minutes for creating and posting content, plus another 20 to 40 minutes for engaging with others. You need 5 to 7 posts weekly minimum. Writing matters more than design or video production skills. Consistency is critical because sporadic posting destroys momentum on X faster than other platforms.

Ask yourself honestly whether you can sustain this investment. Underresourced X presence often delivers worse results than no presence at all because incomplete execution damages credibility. If capacity limitations prevent effective execution, postpone X until resource availability improves or delegate to a team member.

Based on goal alignment and resource assessment, assign X a priority level. Primary platform means 40 to 50 percent of your social media time when your target audience concentrates on X, your goal aligns with platform strengths, and you can commit to daily engagement. Secondary platform means 25 to 35 percent when you have moderate audience overlap and can commit to 3 to 5 posts weekly plus light engagement. Tertiary platform means 10 to 20 percent when you have limited audience overlap and can manage minimal consistent posting. Not prioritized means better to skip X entirely than execute poorly.

Document your decision and rationale. Revisit quarterly as business priorities and platform dynamics evolve.

Baseline Performance Metrics

Metrics provide accountability but require stage appropriate benchmarking. Comparing yourself to accounts with 100,000 followers when you have 500 creates false failure narratives. Understanding what success looks like at your current stage enables realistic goal setting.

For accounts under 1,000 followers, you're in the foundation-building stage. Target 500 to 2,000 impressions per post, which indicates your content reaches beyond immediate followers through engagement and algorithmic distribution. Below 300 impressions suggests content needs improvement or posting frequency needs to increase. Engagement rate should hit 1 to 3 percent, calculated as likes plus replies plus reposts divided by impressions. Below 1 percent suggests content misalignment with audience interests. Above 5 percent indicates strong content market fit. Profile visits should reach 50 to 200 weekly for active accounts. Strong profile visits are a predictor of follower growth. If visits are high but follows are low, profile optimization needs work. Follower growth of 5 to 20 new followers weekly represents healthy sustainable building through content value. Faster growth often comes from viral posts, which are unpredictable, or unsustainable follow and unfollow tactics, which you should avoid.

For accounts between 1,000 and 10,000 followers, you're in the growth stage. Target 2,000 to 10,000 impressions per post. This expanded reach indicates algorithmic amplification and growing network effects. Content improvements should compound. Engagement rates typically decline as follower count grows because not all followers remain equally engaged. Maintaining above 1 percent indicates continued content relevance despite audience growth. Below 0.5 percent suggests content drift or stale approach needing refresh. Follower growth of 50 to 200 weekly shows momentum building. Below 25 weekly may indicate content saturation in your niche requiring strategy evolution.

For accounts above 10,000 followers, you're in the scaling stage. Target 10,000 to 100,000 plus impressions per post since viral potential exists at this scale, though still unpredictable. Consistency matters more than individual post performance. Engagement rates above 0.5 percent are healthy at this scale. Some engagement dilution is natural as audience expands beyond core enthusiasts. Below 0.3 percent suggests significant audience quality issues. Growth patterns shift from consistent weekly additions to more variable patterns influenced by viral moments and algorithm changes.

Establish your baseline by tracking impressions and engagement for your first 30 posts. Calculate median values rather than averages to reduce the impact of outliers. Use your own numbers as benchmarks, not industry standards that may not apply to your niche.

Understanding Platform Dynamics Beyond the Numbers

The statistics tell only part of the story. Understanding how X actually functions day-to-day helps you make better strategic decisions than numbers alone can provide.

The timeline operates on two distinct feeds that serve different purposes. The For You feed uses algorithmic curation to surface content X believes you will find engaging based on your past behavior, accounts you follow, and engagement patterns of similar users. This is where most discovery happens. The Following feed shows chronological posts only from accounts you follow. Most users default to For You, meaning your content competes against the entire platform rather than just against accounts your followers also follow.

This dual-feed reality shapes strategy significantly. Content appearing in For You reaches people who don't follow you yet but share interests with your existing audience. The algorithm promotes your post to similar users when engagement signals suggest value. Strong early engagement from your followers triggers distribution to non-followers. This makes follower quality critical: engaged followers generate the early signals that trigger broader distribution.

Conversation threading makes X unique among social platforms. When you reply to someone, your reply appears both in their notifications and in a threaded conversation visible to anyone viewing the original post. Strategic replies to high-visibility posts expose you to audiences far beyond your followers. A thoughtful reply on a post seen by 100,000 people potentially reaches those 100,000 people even if you have only 500 followers.

Repost and quote dynamics affect your strategy differently. Reposts simply share content with your followers without adding commentary. Quote posts add your perspective while sharing. The algorithm treats these differently: quote posts with substantive commentary often receive broader distribution than simple reposts because they show thought and add value beyond amplification.

The notification system creates engagement patterns worth understanding. Users receive notifications for mentions, replies, likes on their content, reposts, and new followers. Getting into someone's notifications through meaningful engagement creates repeated exposure that pure content posting can't achieve. This makes engagement strategy critical beyond content strategy.

How X Compares to Other Platforms

Understanding X's distinct character helps you allocate resources effectively across platforms.

LinkedIn prioritizes professional content with longer shelf life, so posts remain visible and generating engagement for days rather than hours. The audience expects polished, professional content. Engagement tends toward professional networking rather than casual conversation. X moves faster and rewards more authentic, in-the-moment content.

Instagram prioritizes visual aesthetics. Success requires image and video production capability. The platform doesn't favor text-forward content. If your expertise translates well to visual presentation, Instagram may outperform X. If your value proposition is ideas and analysis rather than visual appeal, X likely serves you better.

TikTok prioritizes entertainment and algorithmic discovery. Even accounts with zero followers can reach millions through strong algorithmic performance. However, the audience skews younger and expects entertainment-oriented content. B2B and professional services often struggle to translate their value proposition to TikTok's entertainment expectations.

Facebook serves established communities and local businesses well through Groups and local business features. Organic reach for business pages has declined dramatically, making Facebook increasingly pay-to-play for business accounts. The audience skews older than X.

Choose platforms based on where your audience actually spends time rather than where you prefer to spend time. Data about your target customer demographics should drive platform prioritization rather than your personal platform preferences.

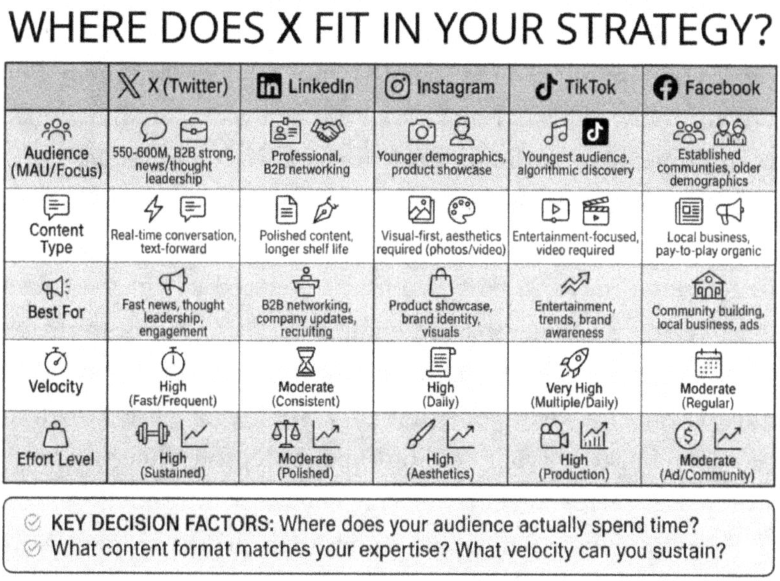

WHERE DOES X FIT IN YOUR STRATEGY?

	X (Twitter)	LinkedIn	Instagram	TikTok	Facebook
Audience (MAU/Focus)	550-600M, B2B strong, news/thought leadership	Professional, B2B networking	Younger demographics, product showcase	Youngest audience, algorithmic discovery	Established communities, older demographics
Content Type	Real-time conversation, text-forward	Polished content, longer shelf life	Visual-first, aesthetics required (photos/video)	Entertainment-focused, video required	Local business, pay-to-play organic
Best For	Fast news, thought leadership, engagement	B2B networking, company updates, recruiting	Product showcase, brand identity, visuals	Entertainment, trends, brand awareness	Community building, local business, ads
Velocity	High (Fast/Frequent)	Moderate (Consistent)	High (Daily)	Very High (Multiple/Daily)	Moderate (Regular)
Effort Level	High (Sustained)	Moderate (Polished)	High (Aesthetics)	High (Production)	Moderate (Ad/Community)

KEY DECISION FACTORS: Where does your audience actually spend time?
What content format matches your expertise? What velocity can you sustain?

Figure 1.1: Platform Comparison Matrix

Premium Subscription Decisions

X offers free accounts, Basic at $3 monthly, Premium at $8 monthly, and Premium Plus at $40 monthly (X Help Center, 2025). The decision matters less than most people think, but understanding the tradeoffs helps allocate resources wisely.

Free tier works fine for most accounts under 10,000 monthly impressions. You can post, engage, build audience, and track basic analytics without paying anything. The main limitations are inability to edit posts after publishing and shorter maximum post length of 280 characters.

Basic tier at $3 monthly includes essential features: editing posts, longer posts up to 25,000 characters (X Help Center, 2025), longer video uploads, reply prioritization, text formatting, and bookmark folders. Basic does NOT include the blue checkmark. Verification requires Premium ($8 monthly) or Premium Plus ($40 monthly). This tier makes sense if you want core functionality improvements without paying for verification or reduced ads.

Premium tier at $8 monthly adds the edit button with a 1 hour window (Inspire to Thrive, 2025; up to 5 edits) to fix typos, longer posts up to 25,000 characters, reduced ads in your feed, and Creator Revenue Sharing eligibility. This becomes valuable when you're posting frequently enough that the edit button saves embarrassment, when you want to write longer posts, when ad reduction improves your reading experience, and when you're approaching Creator Revenue Sharing eligibility thresholds.

Premium Plus at $40 monthly adds reply prioritization so your replies appear higher in threads, largest upload limits, and lowest ad frequency. The February 2025 price increase raised Premium Plus to around $40, linked to Grok 3 AI integration. Check X's Premium page for current pricing as rates continue to evolve. This only makes sense for accounts where reply visibility directly drives business outcomes. At this price point, you need clear ROI justification.

The recommended approach for most businesses is to start free for your first 90 days while testing content market fit. Premium features amplify existing traction better than they create traction from nothing. Once you're consistently hitting 10,000 plus monthly impressions, Premium at $8 monthly makes sense. The top-tier $40/month option only justifies itself for accounts exceeding 100,000 monthly impressions where reply prioritization provides clear business value.

Calculate whether Premium pays for itself with simple math. At $96 annually, Premium needs to generate either 96 additional website visitors if each visitor is worth $1 to you, 24 additional leads if 4 percent of visitors become leads, or one additional client worth more than $96. For most businesses generating any meaningful activity on X, Premium pays for itself easily. If your X presence produces zero business results currently, Premium won't change that. Fix your strategy first.

Putting This Into Practice

Note: The following scenarios illustrate methodology application through composite examples synthesizing patterns from documented implementations. Targets and benchmarks reflect achievable ranges based on published research and case studies cited throughout. Individual results vary based on execution quality, market conditions, audience characteristics, and competitive dynamics.

A Brooklyn coffee shop owner came to this work with 800 followers, sporadic posting, and no clear strategy. Foot traffic was inconsistent and the marketing budget nearly nonexistent. The previous approach was random posting two to three times monthly with no clear voice or strategy. Engagement was minimal with no measurable impact on foot traffic.

The approach was straightforward. Four posts weekly on a consistent Monday, Wednesday, Friday, Saturday schedule. Content organized around four themes serving as content pillars: behind the scenes coffee preparation, coffee education and brewing tips, spotlights on regular customers with their permission, and daily special announcements. Active engagement with the local food community through replies and quote posts on their content. Cross promotion with neighboring businesses through mutual mentions.

The first month focused on establishing posting consistency and defining voice. Months two through three emphasized engagement and relationship building with local accounts. Months four through six saw content refinement based on performance data, doubling down on what worked.

With six months of consistent execution, meaningful follower growth becomes achievable. The targets: measurable foot traffic improvement according to point of sale comparison, trackable customer discovery attribution, with approximately four hours weekly investment. Documented parallels support these targets: Coffee Groundz in Houston achieved 30 percent sales increase and doubled clientele through similar Twitter engagement strategies, and Foster Coffee Company grew to over 15,000 followers with 30 percent year over year growth through consistent content (Buffer, 2018).

The key insight: consistency matters more than frequency. Four high quality posts weekly with genuine engagement outperformed the previous approach of irregular posting without community participation. Behind the scenes content humanized the business and created emotional connection beyond transactional relationship. Community spotlighting generated reciprocal promotion, expanding reach without paid advertising.

A B2B SaaS CEO took a different path toward the same principles. Starting with 450 followers and zero brand presence despite a $2 million product, he needed differentiation in a crowded category competing against established players like Asana and Monday.com. The previous approach focused on product feature announcements, generating minimal engagement.

He began posting three times weekly about industry pain points his product addressed, never mentioning the product directly. He shared his product development journey publicly. He posted controversial but reasoned takes on project management philosophy and industry trends. He shared weekly tactical tips for product managers and team leaders. He created case study threads showing specific customer results with named companies who gave permission. He engaged thoughtfully in product management community conversations, adding substantive commentary rather than promotional replies. He collaborated with other SaaS founders on joint threads discussing bootstrapping, product development, and team building.

The first three months focused on finding voice and testing content types. Months four through six doubled down on highest performing content, which turned out to be controversial takes and case study threads. Months seven through twelve expanded reach through consistent posting and strategic collaboration with complementary accounts.

With twelve months of consistent execution, significant follower growth and pipeline impact become achievable. The targets: meaningful follower growth, substantial increase in demo requests, and attribution tracking showing X discovery as a primary source. The founder voice added authenticity that corporate accounts can't replicate. This pattern mirrors documented B2B results: Avaya closed a $250,000 deal in just 13 days from a single tweet response, showing the pipeline potential when executives engage directly rather than delegating to marketing departments.

The key insight: founder voice adds authenticity that corporate accounts can't replicate. Sharing the journey including mistakes and learnings builds connection stronger than polished marketing messages. Consistent valuable content compounds authority over time, similar to compound interest in investing. Controversial but reasoned takes spark discussion and visibility, though this requires confidence to express opinions publicly. Patience is required because meaningful B2B results take 6 to 12 months minimum, not weeks.

A nonprofit communications director took a different approach, focusing on storytelling about impact rather than donation requests. The strategy emphasized beneficiary outcomes, organizational mission, and behind the scenes glimpses of the work. This mirrors what Charity:water achieved with their Twestival campaign, raising $250,000 in 48 hours across 200+ cities. Research confirms social media engagement correlates with volunteering and donating behavior among nonprofit followers. The pattern holds across different cause areas when content prioritizes impact stories over asks.

A marketing consultant built her practice through consistent X presence over 18 months. She posted three to five times weekly about client challenges and solutions, never naming clients but providing specific enough detail that prospects could see themselves in the scenarios. This approach mirrors what Justin Welsh documented publicly: growing from 2,000 to over 750,000 followers while generating $10.3 million in revenue with 86 percent margins through consistent content. The revenue comes not from virality but from sustained presence that builds trust over time.

None of these results came from tricks or hacks. They came from understanding where X fits strategically, showing up consistently, and measuring what actually matters. With platform fit established, the next step is optimizing your presence, starting with the foundational asset: your profile.

| 2 |

Setting Up Your Professional X Profile

Inside This Chapter

We examine every element of your X profile and how each converts visitors to followers. The analysis covers profile photo specifications, header image strategy, bio writing within the 160 character constraint, and pinned post optimization. It documents the psychology of three second decisions and the specific changes that improve conversion rates significantly.

Someone clicks through to your X profile from a post or conversation. They spend three seconds scanning your photo, header, and bio before deciding whether to follow. Three seconds to convert curiosity into commitment. Your profile either communicates clear value or creates confusion. No middle ground.

Why Profile Completion Matters

Your X profile functions as a landing page. Users arrive from various sources. They see your post in their feed and want to know more. You reply to their content and they check you out. Someone mentions you and they investigate. They discover you through search on a topic you discuss. Each source brings visitors with different intent levels, but all make the same snap judgment about whether to follow.

Complete profiles convert significantly more visitors to followers than incomplete profiles. Establish your own baseline by dividing new followers by profile visits over a 30-day period, then measure improvement after optimization. Incomplete profiles convert significantly less because each missing or weak element creates friction in the decision.

Profile photos create recognition and trust. Headers communicate positioning at a glance. Bios explain who you serve and what problems you solve. Location provides geographic context for local businesses and establishes credibility for others. Website links drive traffic to owned properties where conversion happens. Pinned posts showcase your best work and current priorities. The sum of these elements either compels follows or enables quick exits.

Incomplete profiles raise questions that prevent follows because missing photos suggest abandoned accounts or bots while generic headers waste premium visual real estate and vague bios force visitors to investigate rather than following immediately. Each incomplete element creates friction that reduces conversion.

The strategy: complete all profile elements in a single optimization session this week. Track profile completion in X settings and target 100 percent. Monitor weekly profile visits and calculate your follow conversion rate in X Analytics by dividing new followers by profile visits. Track your baseline before optimization, then measure improvement after changes. If your conversion rate falls below 10 percent, profile optimization likely needs work before content strategy will pay off.

Profile Photo Strategy

Profile photos appear everywhere on X. They show in feeds at 48 by 48 pixels when people scroll past your posts, in profiles at 200 by 200 pixels when people visit, and in notifications at various sizes. The platform displays them as circles, cropping square images to circular format. Understanding these display contexts shapes optimal photo selection.

Technical specifications matter for quality display. Profile photos need 400 by 400 pixel minimum resolution, under 2MB file size, in JPG or PNG format. Upload photos exceeding minimum resolution to ensure clarity when scaled down. Test circular crop before uploading to confirm critical elements stay visible and nothing important gets clipped at the edges.

For personal brands, professional headshots work best with faces occupying 60 to 80 percent of the frame. This facial emphasis enables recognition at small sizes in busy feeds. Friendly expression with direct eye contact builds trust. Lighting should illuminate your face clearly. Background shouldn't distract. Avoid group photos where you can't be immediately identified. Avoid logos or graphics instead of faces for personal brands because people connect with people.

For business brands, use your primary logo with sufficient padding to remain visible at 48 by 48 pixels. Complex logos with fine details often become illegible at small sizes, requiring simplified versions. If your full logo doesn't read clearly at small sizes, use an icon or simplified mark instead. Ensure brand colors are preserved accurately.

Use the same photo across LinkedIn, Instagram, Facebook, and your website. Cross platform consistency amplifies recognition significantly. Users encountering your content across platforms recognize identical photos faster, building familiarity and trust. One strategic photo selection multiplies value everywhere you appear online.

The goal with your profile photo is immediate recognition and appropriate trust signals. Within one second of seeing your photo, visitors should have a clear sense of who they're looking at. Track whether your current photo achieves this by asking three people unfamiliar with your brand to describe their impression after seeing only your profile photo for two seconds.

Header Image Strategy

Headers occupy the largest visual space on your profile. At 1500 by 500 pixels, they provide billboard style real estate for communicating value proposition, showcasing work, or reinforcing positioning. Most accounts waste this space with generic stock photos or leave it blank entirely.

Mobile devices crop headers differently than desktop, which creates a design challenge. The safe zone measures 1200 by 400 pixels centered within the full canvas. All critical information including text, key visuals, and brand elements must stay within this safe zone to display properly on both desktop and mobile views.

Different account types benefit from different header approaches. Consultants and service providers should feature taglines summarizing expertise plus credentials or social proof. Use 80 to 120 point font minimum for legibility. Example: "B2B Marketing Strategy" plus "Trusted by 40+ SaaS companies" plus logos of recognizable clients.

Product companies should show hero products in use or dashboard screenshots showing key benefits. Seeing the product builds familiarity before prospects ever click through to your website. Feature the primary use case or most compelling capability.

Creators and media personalities should display recent work grids or signature content formats. If you create videos, show video thumbnails. If you write, show article headlines. Let visitors immediately understand what content they will get by following.

Personal brands should combine professional photos with value proposition text, using different photos than profile pictures to avoid redundancy. The combination humanizes while communicating what you offer.

Design at exactly 1500 by 500 pixels. Export at 72 DPI for web display. Keep files under 2MB for fast loading. Use PNG format for graphics with text because it preserves sharp edges. Use JPEG format for photographic backgrounds.

Test your header by viewing your profile on mobile device and asking whether the key message is clear. If critical elements are cropped or text is unreadable, redesign within the safe zone.

Bio Writing in 160 Characters

Your bio must communicate what you do, who you serve, and why someone should care, all within 160 characters. This constraint forces clarity that benefits everyone. Vague bios that waste this space with filler phrases forfeit the most valuable text on your profile.

The three part formula works reliably. First, state what you do in specific terms. Marketing consultant beats entrepreneur. B2B SaaS growth strategist beats business helper. Specificity attracts qualified followers while generic labels attract everyone and therefore no one. Second, identify who you serve. Small business owners, enterprise sales teams, nonprofit communications directors. This qualification helps potential followers self select. Third, add a proof point. Years of experience, specific client results, credentials, or media mentions. This element builds credibility for your claims.

Example transformation: "Entrepreneur and business enthusiast helping companies grow" becomes "B2B marketing strategist | Helping SaaS companies turn LinkedIn into pipeline | Ex-HubSpot | 40+ clients served". The second version communicates specific expertise, target client, credibility signal, and track record in the same character count.

Character optimization matters when space is tight. Remove articles like the, a, and an. Use ampersands instead of and. Use numerals instead of spelled numbers. Cut filler phrases like helping you or passionate about. Use vertical bars or bullets as separators rather than sentences. Every character should earn its place.

Include two to three keywords your target audience might search. X's search function indexes bios, so including relevant terms helps discovery. If you help SaaS companies with LinkedIn strategy, include SaaS and LinkedIn. If you consult on nonprofit fundraising, include nonprofit and fundraising. Think about what someone looking for your services would type into search.

Test different bio versions monthly and track which bios correlate with higher follow conversion rates. Small changes compound over time. A bio improvement that increases conversion by

2 percentage points means 20 additional followers per 1,000 profile visitors.

Pinned Post Strategy

Pinned posts stay fixed at the top of your profile regardless of new content. This prime real estate should work harder than any other single post because every profile visitor sees it first.

Use pinned posts strategically for your current priority. For lead generation, link to your email signup, free resource, or consultation booking page. Include clear description of what visitors get and explicit call to action. For showcasing expertise, pin your best performing thread or most valuable insight. Let your strongest work make the first impression. For promoting current offers, pin launches, events, or limited opportunities. Update as promotions change.

The most effective pinned posts combine value with conversion opportunity. Rather than just announcing "Book a consultation" which provides no value, show expertise while offering next steps: a thread showing your strategic framework followed by an offer to apply it to the reader's situation.

Update pinned posts when priorities change. Launching a new service? Pin the announcement. Running a promotion? Pin the details. Have a thread that performed exceptionally? Pin it to extend its productive life. A stale pinned post signals an inactive or unfocused account.

Include clear calls to action. Tell visitors exactly what to do next. Sign up, download, book, or read more. Specific verbs outperform vague suggestions. "Download the free template" outperforms "Check it out if interested."

Track pinned post performance through link clicks if your pin includes a link. Compare click through rates across different pinned posts to identify what resonates with your audience.

Location and Website Fields

Beyond the primary profile elements, location and website fields provide additional optimization opportunities often overlooked.

Location field serves different purposes for different account types. Local businesses should include specific geographic location to attract local audience and appear in location-based searches. Service area rather than office address works if you serve a region: "Serving Greater Boston" rather than a specific street address.

Remote businesses and personal brands have more flexibility. Options include: city name establishing geographic context and relatability, "Remote" or "Everywhere" signaling location-independence, leaving blank if location is irrelevant to value proposition, or using location playfully if it fits brand voice.

Website field should link to your highest-value conversion point, not necessarily your homepage. If email signup drives more business value than general website traffic, link directly to signup page. If booking consultations matters most, link to scheduling page. If selling products, link to product page or store.

Test different landing pages periodically by changing the link and tracking conversion differences over 30 to 60 days. The website field is prime real estate. Optimize it based on data rather than default assumptions.

Consider using a link aggregator like Linktree only if you genuinely have multiple equally important destinations. Single focused links typically outperform link aggregators because they reduce friction and decision fatigue. Aggregators work when you genuinely need to offer choices.

Profile Photo Psychology

Profile photos communicate more than identity. They establish trust, approachability, and professionalism through subtle signals most users don't consciously process.

Facial expression matters significantly. Genuine smiles showing some teeth outperform serious expressions for most business contexts. The smile should reach your eyes: forced smiles read as insincere even in small photos. Friendly expression lowers barriers to engagement.

Eye contact with camera creates connection. Looking directly at the lens feels like looking at the viewer. Looking away feels distant or distracted. Direct eye contact increases follow rates in testing across multiple accounts.

Color choices affect visibility and recognition. Solid colored backgrounds make faces stand out. Busy backgrounds compete for attention and reduce face recognition at small sizes. Consider how your photo appears against X's interface: avoid colors that blend with the platform's blue and white design.

Consistency across changes matters. When updating your photo, maintain similar framing, color palette, and overall feel so followers recognize you. Dramatic photo changes can cause recognition confusion until followers adjust.

Bio Testing Framework

Systematic bio testing reveals what actually works for your specific audience rather than relying on generic best practices that may not apply.

Establish baseline metrics before testing: follow conversion rate calculated as new followers divided by profile visits over a defined period, typically 30 days. Track this consistently using X Analytics.

Change one element at a time so you can attribute any changes to specific modifications. Running multiple tests simultaneously prevents learning which change drove results.

Test duration should be minimum 14 days, ideally 30 days, to accumulate sufficient data for meaningful comparison. Short tests may reflect random variation rather than actual performance differences.

Elements worth testing include: credential placement (leading with credentials versus ending with them), specificity level (narrow niche description versus broader expertise claim), social proof type (client count versus results claims versus credentials), call to action presence (direct CTA versus no CTA), and tone (professional versus conversational versus playful).

Document all tests and results to build institutional knowledge. What works for your audience becomes clearer over multiple tests.

Putting This Into Practice

A marketing consultant with five years experience had 1,800 followers and sporadic inbound leads. Her profile had a generic header showing a stock photo of a laptop, a vague bio, and no pinned post. Profile visits averaged 150 weekly but follow conversion lagged her potential.

She redesigned everything in one focused three hour session. New header featuring her tagline "B2B Marketing Strategy" in large readable text, with four client logos showing social proof, designed within the mobile safe zone. Bio rewritten to "B2B marketing strategist | Helping SaaS companies turn LinkedIn into pipeline | Ex-HubSpot | 40+ clients served" communicating specific expertise, target market, credibility signal, and track record. Pinned post linking to her free LinkedIn audit template with clear signup call to action and description of what subscribers would receive.

The targets for this optimization: profile visits doubling within 60 days, follow conversion improving from single digits toward the 20+ percent range, and meaningful email list growth from pinned post conversions. With consistent execution, these improvements can translate to significant new retainer business. B2B patterns support these targets when consultants optimize profile elements systematically. Track your baseline conversion rate and measure improvement over 60 to 90 days.

The transformation required no additional posting or content creation. The same content volume suddenly converted far better because the profile made clear value immediately apparent.

A SaaS company had 3,400 followers but struggled to communicate product value. Their header showed a generic office stock photo that could belong to any company. Bio read "Building the future of work" which sounds impressive but communicates nothing specific. Visitors had no idea what the company actually did without clicking through to investigate further, which most wouldn't do.

They replaced the header with a product dashboard screenshot showing their key differentiator, the specific feature that distinguished them from competitors. Visitors could immediately see what the product did. Bio became "Project management for remote teams | Async-first collaboration | Used by 500+ companies | Free trial: yoursite.com/trial" communicating the product category, key differentiator, social proof, and call to action. Pinned post featured a customer testimonial thread with specific results: "How [Company] reduced meeting time 40% using [Product]."

The goal: significantly increase demo requests within 90 days through profile optimization alone. Well-optimized profiles can achieve conversion rates substantially higher than paid channels because visitors arrive pre-educated through content consumption. B2B research from MarTech confirms profile optimization directly correlates with demo conversion rates.

A nonprofit communications director transformed an underperforming profile into a donation driver. Previous bio mentioned organization name but not mission or impact. Header showed office building exterior, which communicated nothing about the cause. No pinned post was set.

She rewrote the bio to focus on impact: "Helping 2,000+ families access affordable housing annually | Stories of hope and transformation | Donate: yourorg.com/donate" communicating scale, mission, emotional appeal, and direct call to action. New header featured a beneficiary photo, with permission, with overlay text showing key statistics: "2,000 families housed | 15 years | Your donation at work." Pinned post linked to current campaign with specific funding goal, progress thermometer, and impact description.

The target: triple profile conversion rate through optimization. A well-crafted pinned post can generate meaningful donation traffic. [Individual results vary.]

| 3 |

Understanding X Premium & Verification

Inside This Chapter

We examine X's subscription tiers and whether any of them deserve your money. The analysis covers Basic, Premium, and Premium Plus features, costs, and business value calculations. It documents Creator Revenue Sharing eligibility requirements and realistic income expectations. The chapter provides frameworks for calculating whether subscription costs generate positive return on investment for your specific situation.

X wants you to pay for Premium. The platform surfaces upgrade prompts constantly. Blue checkmarks appear everywhere, creating social pressure to join. Before spending money, understand what you actually get and whether it justifies the cost for your specific situation.

The Four Tiers Explained

X operates four account tiers with distinct feature sets and price points.

Free accounts cost nothing and provide basic posting, engagement, and analytics access. You can build a meaningful presence without paying anything. The main limitations are inability to edit posts after publishing, which means typos require deleting and reposting, and shorter maximum post length of 280 characters, which constrains longer form content to threads.

Basic tier costs $3 monthly and includes essential features: editing posts, longer posts up to 25,000 characters, longer video uploads, reply prioritization, text formatting, and bookmark folders. Basic does NOT include the blue checkmark. The checkmark requires Premium or Premium Plus subscription. This tier makes sense for accounts wanting core functionality improvements without paying for verification.

Premium tier costs $8 monthly when purchased through web browser or $11 monthly through mobile app stores which take a cut. Premium adds the edit button with a 1 hour window (up to 5 edits) to fix posts after publishing, longer posts up to 25,000 characters enabling detailed single posts rather than threads for moderate length content, reduced ads in your reading experience, and Creator Revenue Sharing eligibility allowing you to earn from engagement on your content.

Premium Plus tier costs $40 monthly following the February 2025 price increase from $16. This 150 percent price jump reflected Grok 3 AI integration. Premium Plus adds reply prioritization meaning your replies appear higher in threads than non Premium Plus accounts, largest upload limits for video and media, and lowest ad frequency in your feed.

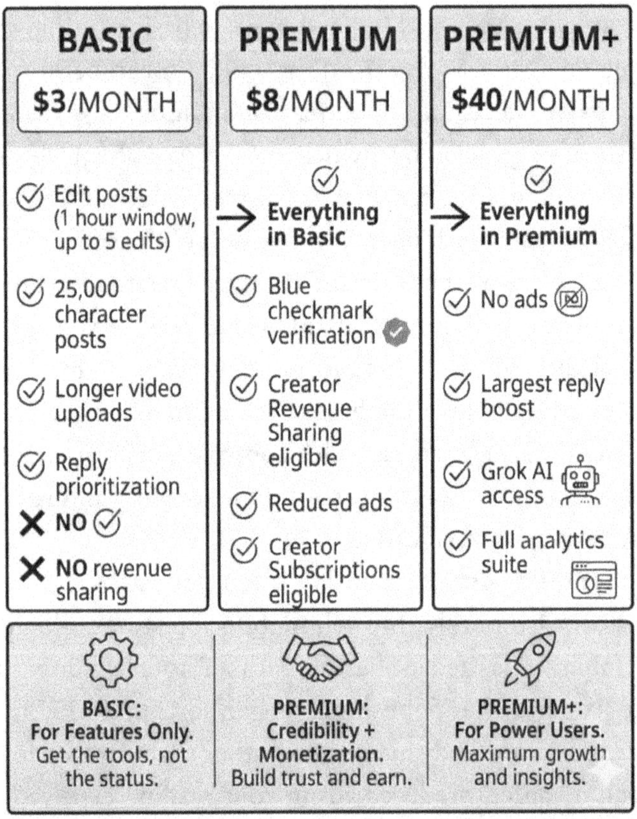

Ai Generated by Gemini

Figure 3.1: X Premium Tiers Comparison

The Edit Button Reality

Premium and Premium Plus subscribers can edit posts within 1 hour of publishing, with up to 5 edits allowed within that window. This lets you fix typos, correct errors, and refine phrasing without deleting and reposting. The limitation is meaningful: after 1 hour, posts become permanent like they were before the edit feature existed.

The edit button matters more for some accounts than others. High volume posters who publish multiple times daily benefit because more posts mean more opportunities for typos. Professional brands where errors damage credibility benefit because one embarrassing typo can undermine positioning. Public figures benefit because mistakes get screenshotted and amplified before you can fix them.

The edit button matters less for casual posters publishing a few times weekly, accounts where authenticity outweighs polish and followers appreciate imperfection, and situations where you can simply delete and repost without consequence.

Calculate your typo cost honestly. If errors damage your professional reputation or require awkward correction posts that call attention to mistakes, the edit button has meaningful value. If typos just make you human and your audience doesn't mind, save the money until posting volume increases.

Creator Revenue Sharing

Premium and Premium Plus unlock eligibility for Creator Revenue Sharing, but eligibility doesn't guarantee meaningful income. The program has specific requirements and realistic income expectations worth understanding before treating it as business strategy.

Requirements for eligibility include 2,000 verified followers meaning you need Premium or Premium Plus subscription first, plus 5 million impressions over the past three months. These thresholds change frequently, so verify current requirements at help.x.com before planning monetization strategy. The impression threshold excludes most small accounts. Five million impressions over three months means averaging roughly 1.7 million monthly impressions, or about 55,000 daily. Most business accounts with under 10,000 followers generate nowhere near this volume.

Revenue comes from ads displayed in reply threads under your posts. When someone replies to your post and ads appear in that reply thread, you earn a portion of ad revenue. Distribution happens biweekly via Stripe. You should set up Stripe account to receive payments.

The math rarely favors small accounts. At minimum threshold of 5 million impressions quarterly, creator reports suggest earnings of roughly $50 to $300 monthly depending on your content niche and audience demographics, though results vary widely. Technology and business audiences command higher ad rates than general entertainment. Reaching $1,000 monthly requires sustained high engagement with large audiences, typically 20,000 plus engaged followers generating consistent viral or near viral content.

Creator Revenue Sharing makes sense as bonus income for accounts already generating high engagement naturally. It doesn't make sense as primary motivation for Premium subscription. For most business accounts, indirect monetization through leads, clients, and business development generates far more value than platform payments ever will.

Calculating Premium ROI

Premium costs $96 annually at the $8 monthly rate. For that investment to make sense, X activity needs to generate at least $96 in business value that wouldn't occur without Premium features.

Work backward from your numbers to determine break even. If your average website visitor is worth $1 in eventual revenue, Premium needs to generate 96 additional visitors. If 4 percent of website visitors become leads, Premium needs to generate 24 additional leads to break even. If your average client value is $500, Premium needs to generate 0.2 clients, meaning one client every five years covers the cost entirely.

For most businesses generating any meaningful activity on X, Premium pays for itself easily within these calculations. The question is whether you're generating that activity yet. If your X presence produces zero business results currently, Premium won't change that. The features amplify existing traction better than they create traction from nothing. Fix your strategy first, then add Premium to accelerate.

Premium Plus requires more careful calculation at $480 annually, five times the cost of regular Premium. The primary benefit is reply prioritization, meaning your replies appear higher in threads than non Premium Plus accounts. This matters if replies drive your discovery and business development. If you spend significant time replying to high profile accounts and those replies generate profile visits and leads, higher placement could meaningfully impact results. For most accounts, it doesn't justify 5x the cost of regular Premium.

The test for Premium Plus is simple: does reply visibility directly correlate with your business outcomes? If yes and you can document the correlation, run a 90 day test comparing baseline metrics before upgrade against metrics after. If no clear correlation exists between reply placement and business results, save the $384 annual difference.

The 90-Day Test Protocol

When uncertain whether Premium tiers justify their cost, run a structured test rather than guessing.

Pre-test documentation (Week 0): Before upgrading, document current baseline metrics you can measure against post-upgrade performance. Record average impressions per post over past 30 days. Record engagement rate average. Record profile visits per week. Record any business metrics you can attribute to X: leads, inquiries, sales. This baseline documentation enables meaningful comparison.

Test execution (Weeks 1 through 12): Upgrade to the tier you're testing. Maintain posting strategy and frequency consistent with pre-test period to isolate tier effects, then track the same metrics weekly that you documented in baseline.

Post-test analysis (Week 13): Compare test period metrics against baseline. Calculate improvement percentages. Multiply improvements by business value to estimate ROI. Compare ROI against subscription cost. Make retention decision based on data rather than assumption.

Common test findings: Most accounts testing Premium from free see meaningful improvement in content management through edit button and longer posts, modest to no improvement in business metrics because Premium features amplify rather than create traction. Accounts testing Premium Plus from Premium see improvement only if their strategy depends on reply visibility.

Verification and Checkmarks Explained

The verification checkmark system has evolved significantly. Understanding current dynamics helps you decide whether verification matters for your goals.

Blue checkmarks now indicate paid subscription rather than identity verification as they did historically. Premium and Premium Plus subscribers receive a checkmark, meaning checkmarks no longer signal notable accounts as they once did.

Gold checkmarks indicate verified organizations that have completed business verification through X's process, requiring documentation proving business legitimacy. Gold checkmarks signal organizational accounts rather than individual accounts.

Gray checkmarks indicate government or multilateral organization accounts with institutional verification.

Strategic implications: Blue checkmarks provide some credibility signal but less than historical verified status. Some audiences remain impressed by checkmarks. Others recognize they indicate payment rather than notability. Industry context matters: professional services may benefit more from checkmark credibility than creative or entertainment accounts.

For most business accounts, the features bundled with Premium justify the subscription regardless of checkmark value. The checkmark is a minor bonus rather than primary reason to subscribe.

Putting This Into Practice

One business consultant found Premium Plus justified the upgrade from regular Premium. She was already hitting 200,000 monthly impressions and used replies to high visibility conversations as her primary discovery mechanism. Her strategy involved adding thoughtful commentary to trending industry discussions, positioning her expertise where attention already concentrated.

She ran a documented 90 day test. Before upgrading, she documented her baseline across multiple metrics: replies appeared at lower positions in busy threads with 50 plus responses based on manual sampling, profile visits from reply activity and qualified business inquiries were modest attributable to X discovery.

After upgrading to Premium Plus, she tracked the same metrics carefully. Reply positions improved significantly in equivalent threads. Increased profile visits from reply engagement. Growth in qualified inquiries. Course and consulting sales attributed to X discovery showed meaningful growth.

The $40 monthly cost generated $2,600 monthly in incremental revenue based on the before and after comparison. For her specific business model where reply visibility drove discovery, Premium Plus delivered meaningful return on investment. The upgrade proved worthwhile for her specific situation.

But another account, a digital marketing agency, ran the same test with completely different results. They canceled after 90 days. Despite 12,000 followers and strong engagement metrics, their business development did not depend on reply visibility. Their leads came from direct content discovery rather than reply threads. Profile visits increased only 12 percent with Premium Plus versus baseline. Business inquiries showed no statistically significant change. The $480 annual cost produced no measurable return because their business model did not align with the specific features Premium Plus provides.

The lesson isn't that Premium Plus works or doesn't work universally. The lesson is that subscription value depends entirely on your specific business model and how X fits your customer acquisition process. Run your own test if reply visibility seems strategically important. Skip Premium Plus if your discovery happens through content rather than replies. Neither answer is correct for everyone.

| 4 |

Content Strategy and Planning

Inside This Chapter

We examine the systems that transform sporadic posting into sustainable growth. The analysis covers content pillar frameworks that organize your expertise into recognizable themes, the 70/30 planning rule that balances scheduled consistency with reactive engagement, and batching workflows that create weeks of content in focused sessions rather than daily scrambling.

Every Monday morning, someone opens a blank document and stares at it. Their business coach said X could generate leads with consistent posting. They downloaded three content calendar templates. Two weeks later, nothing has changed. They post sporadically when inspiration strikes, usually while scrolling at 11 PM and second guessing every word. Followers stagnate. The templates sit unused. Most small business owners fail at X not because they lack expertise but because they lack systems that convert intention into execution. This chapter provides those systems.

Content Pillars Create Structure

Random posting creates random results. Successful X strategies require planned content architecture balanced with reactive engagement capacity.

The data supports this approach clearly. Brands posting consistently five to seven times weekly grow followers three times faster than sporadic posters. Content calendars prevent random posting while allowing flexibility for trending topics and real time conversations. The goal isn't rigid adherence to a schedule that ignores what is happening in the world, but systematic consistency that ensures you show up regularly.

Establish three to five content pillars representing your core expertise areas. Content pillars are the recurring themes your audience comes to expect from you. They create coherence across posts and help audiences understand your value proposition quickly.

A marketing consultant might allocate pillars as follows: Strategy and Planning at 30 percent covering frameworks, goal setting, and positioning discussions; Execution and Tactics at 30 percent covering specific how-to content and implementation guidance; Case Studies at 20 percent showing real results and client transformations; Industry Trends at 10 percent commenting on news and changes in the marketing field; and Personal Insights at 10 percent sharing journey, lessons learned, and behind the scenes perspective.

A SaaS company might structure differently: Productivity Tips at 35 percent providing value to their target users regardless of product adoption; Product Updates at 25 percent keeping existing users informed and showing ongoing development; Customer Success at 20 percent showcasing how real companies use the product; Remote Work Trends at 15 percent establishing broader thought leadership in their space; and Company Culture at 5 percent humanizing the brand and supporting recruitment.

More than five pillars creates inconsistent positioning because you can't give each sufficient attention. Audiences can't remember what you stand for when topics scatter too widely. Fewer than three pillars limits content variety and risks boring your audience with repetitive messaging. The sweet spot balances variety that keeps followers engaged with focus that builds clear positioning.

The tactical implementation starts with generating 20 post ideas per pillar before building your calendar. This content bank prevents the blank page problem that causes calendar abandonment. Include multiple content types within each pillar: tips, questions, case studies, data points, controversial opinions, and how-to guidance. When you sit down to create content, you select from existing ideas rather than generating from scratch.

Track pillar balance monthly to ensure you're delivering on your positioning promise. Count posts per pillar and compare to target percentages. If pillars drift more than 10 percent from targets for two consecutive months, your audience receives inconsistent value signaling unclear positioning. Rebalance by generating more content in underrepresented pillars.

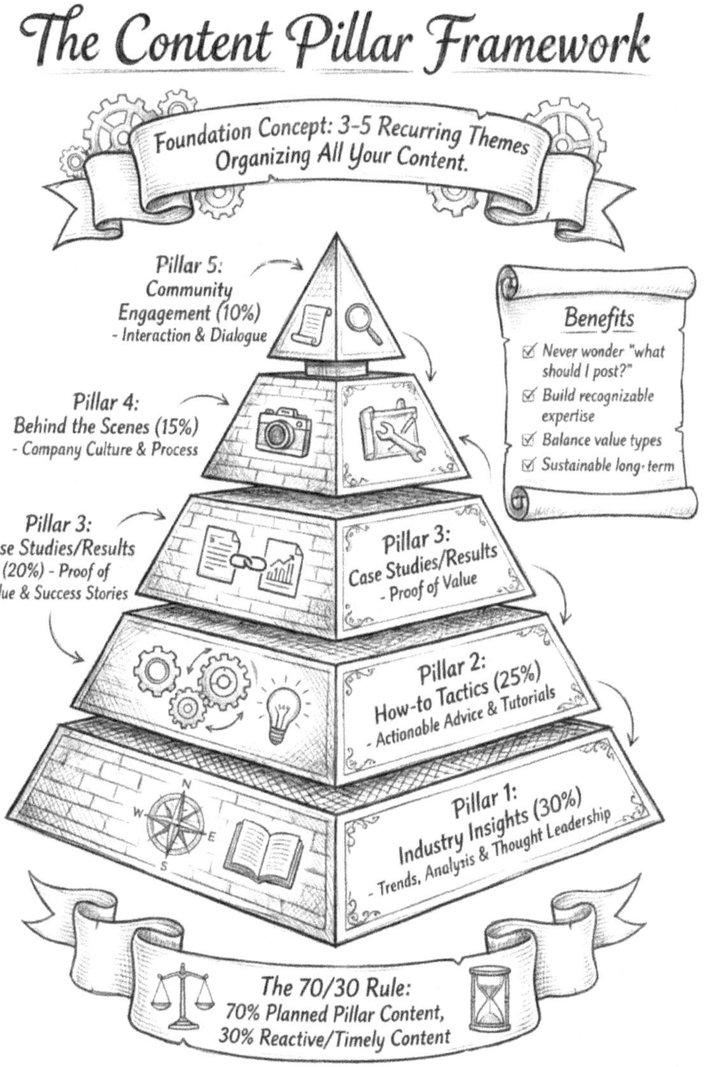

Figure 4.1: The Content Pillar Framework

The 70/30 Planning Rule

Plan 70 percent of content in advance through scheduled posts and pillar aligned material. Reserve 30 percent capacity for reactive content including trending topics, real time engagement, and spontaneous thoughts. This balance maintains consistency while preserving agility for cultural moments.

The data supports this split. Marketers using weekly scheduling report 76 percent increased engagement year over year compared to those posting reactively. Scheduled content ensures consistent presence during busy periods, vacation, or unforeseen circumstances. This reliability builds audience trust and algorithmic favor because the platform rewards accounts that show up consistently.

But pure scheduling creates problems too. A 100 percent scheduled account feels robotic and misses opportunities to participate in timely conversations that drive discovery. The 30 percent reactive capacity enables joining trending discussions, responding to news in your industry, and participating in conversations that couldn't be predicted when you created your content calendar.

Measure your reactive versus planned ratio monthly by tagging posts in your tracking system and calculating distribution. If reactive content exceeds 50 percent, your strategy lacks sufficient structure and you're probably scrambling more than necessary. If planned content exceeds 90 percent, your presence feels robotic and you are missing trending opportunities that could expand reach.

The goal: hitting both targets: consistent presence through planning and human connection through reactive engagement. Neither extreme serves you well.

Batching Creates Efficiency

Monthly batching creates greater efficiency than daily scrambling. Context switching costs mean daily creation often takes twice as long cumulatively as focused batching sessions. When you sit down to create content daily, you spend time getting into creative mode, then getting interrupted, then getting back into creative mode. Batching eliminates this cycle.

Dedicate one three hour session monthly to generate 20 to 30 posts covering your 70 percent planned content. Block this time on your calendar as a non-negotiable appointment. Monday or Tuesday of the first week works well because it sets up the month ahead.

The batching session follows a structure optimized through trial and error. First, 30 minutes: review last month's analytics and identify top performing content patterns. What topics resonated? What formats drove engagement? What underperformed? This analysis informs what to create more of and what to abandon. Next, 90 minutes: generate new content across all pillars using your content bank as starting point. Work through each pillar systematically, selecting ideas from your bank and drafting posts. Final 60 minutes: schedule posts in your chosen tool and organize the calendar for the month ahead, ensuring pillar balance across weeks.

Weekly 30 minute planning sessions supplement monthly batching. Review upcoming week's scheduled content to ensure nothing feels stale or poorly timed given current events. Identify gaps where reactive content might slot in. Add posts based on current trends and ensure pillar balance stays on target for the week.

Calendar adherence serves as a key metric. Track scheduled posts actually published divided by posts planned. Target 85 percent or higher monthly adherence. Below 70 percent indicates overambitious planning requiring volume reduction. Above 95 percent suggests excessive rigidity leaving no room for opportunistic content. When adherence drops, reduce planned volume rather than abandoning the calendar entirely. Sustainability beats ambition.

Step-by-Step Monthly Batching Process

The batching session follows a specific structure optimized through extensive trial and error. This level of detail may seem excessive, but following the process precisely prevents the session drift that causes batching to fail.

Week One, Day One: Schedule a three-hour block with no meetings before or after. Don't batch during fragmented time. Prepare your workspace by closing email, silencing phone, and opening only the tools you need: analytics dashboard, content bank document, and scheduling tool.

First 30 minutes: Analytics Review. Open X Analytics and examine the past 30 days. Note your top five performing posts by engagement rate rather than raw impressions. What topics were they? What format? What time were they posted? Note your bottom five performers. What can you learn from the contrast? Update your content bank based on insights: add new ideas inspired by winners, remove or revise ideas similar to losers.

Minutes 30 to 45: Pillar Audit. Count posts from last month by pillar. Calculate actual percentages against targets. If Strategy content was supposed to be 30 percent but was actually 45 percent, you need to generate more content in other pillars this month. Document needed rebalancing.

Minutes 45 to 60: Idea Selection. Review your content bank and select 20 to 25 ideas for the coming month. Ensure pillar balance in your selections. Mark selected ideas as "in progress" so you don't accidentally select them again next month.

Minutes 60 to 150: Drafting. This is the core creative work. Work through selected ideas one by one, drafting complete posts. Don't edit excessively during drafting. Get ideas down, then refine. Aim for 15 to 20 complete draft posts. Some ideas won't work once you try to write them. That is normal. Skip those and move on.

Minutes 150 to 180: Scheduling and Organization. Upload completed drafts to your scheduling tool. Assign posting times based on your analytics data about when engagement peaks, then review the calendar view to ensure variety: don't schedule similar posts on consecutive days. Verify pillar balance across weeks.

After the session: Send yourself a quick summary noting how many posts you created, any ideas that did not work out, and topics to research before next month's session. This note becomes your starting point next month.

Content Bank Development

Your content bank is a living document containing post ideas organized by pillar. This bank prevents the blank page problem that causes most content planning to fail.

Create a simple document or spreadsheet with columns for: Pillar, Post Idea, Content Type (tip, question, opinion, case study, etc.), Status (bank, in progress, posted), and Notes.

Populate initially by brainstorming 20 ideas per pillar. This takes two to three hours but needs to happen only once. Subsequent sessions maintain and draw from the bank rather than starting fresh.

Add to the bank whenever inspiration strikes. See a question your audience would find interesting? Add it to the bank. Read an article with a provocative point? Add your reaction to the bank. Notice a pattern in client conversations? Add it to the bank. Capture ideas when they occur rather than trying to remember them during batching sessions.

Review and prune quarterly. Some ideas age poorly. Some ideas you will never actually write. Remove stale ideas to keep the bank relevant and manageable.

Putting This Into Practice

A local coffee roaster had been posting randomly for two years with minimal growth. Some weeks saw five posts, others saw zero. Content jumped between product photos, coffee education, random thoughts, and occasional promotions with no discernible pattern. Followers grew slowly and engagement remained inconsistent.

She implemented a simple pillar structure: Coffee Education at 40 percent covering brewing techniques, bean origins, and coffee science; Behind the Scenes at 30 percent showing roasting process, daily operations, and the craft involved; Customer Spotlights at 20 percent featuring regulars and their stories with permission; and Local Community at 10 percent highlighting neighborhood events and neighboring businesses.

Monthly batching sessions on the first Sunday of each month generated all scheduled content for the weeks ahead. She reserved 30 percent capacity for spontaneous posts about daily specials, weather-related content, or community events that couldn't be predicted in advance.

With consistent batched posting over four to six months, meaningful follower growth becomes achievable. More importantly, batching typically reduces total time spent because it replaces daily scrambling with systematic sessions. Documented parallel: Foster Coffee Company grew to over 15,000 followers with 30 percent year over year growth through consistent batched content (Buffer, 2018).

A B2B SaaS founder struggled with the opposite problem. His content calendar was packed with scheduled posts, but everything felt stale and disconnected from current conversations. He was hitting 95 percent planned content with almost no reactive engagement. His account felt like a broadcasting machine rather than a participating member of his industry community.

He adjusted to the 70/30 rule, reducing scheduled posts and deliberately leaving gaps for trending topic responses. He started participating in industry conversations through replies and quote tweets rather than just publishing his own content. He would see a discussion about remote work challenges and add his perspective rather than waiting to post his scheduled productivity tip.

Engagement rates increased 34 percent within 60 days as his account felt more human and connected to what was actually happening in his space. More importantly, the reactive engagement introduced him to accounts he would never have reached through scheduled broadcasting alone.

| 5 |

Writing Posts & Threads That Perform

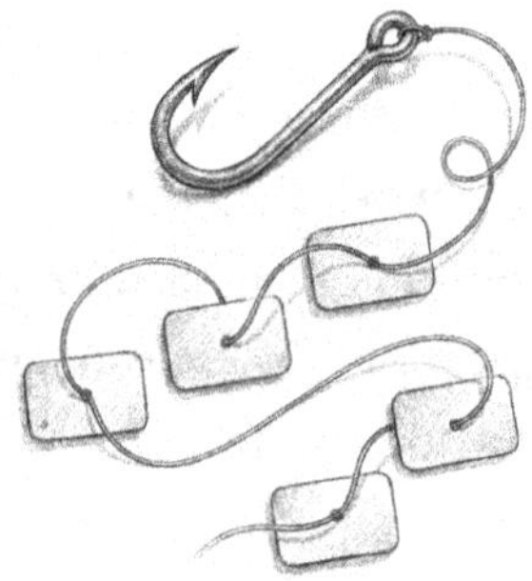

Inside This Chapter

We examine the specific writing techniques that separate posts people scroll past from posts that stop thumbs and generate engagement. The analysis covers hook formulas that create curiosity and promise value, thread structures that sustain attention across multiple tweets, and language patterns that drive replies rather than passive consumption.

Your post appears in a feed alongside hundreds of others. The reader is scrolling fast, attention fragmented, looking for something worth stopping for. You have about two seconds to earn their pause. The hook either works or your carefully crafted insight disappears into the void.

Hooks That Stop Scrolling

The first line determines everything. Strong hooks create curiosity gaps, challenge assumptions, or promise specific value. Weak hooks get scrolled past regardless of how valuable the content that follows.

Curiosity gaps work by opening a question the reader needs answered. The technique creates tension between what is stated and what is unknown. "I spent $50,000 on X ads before learning this" creates immediate need to know what was learned. "The engagement hack everyone talks about actually destroys your account" demands explanation. The reader can't scroll past without resolving the opened question.

The tactical application is straightforward: identify the core insight of your post, then craft an opening that hints at the insight without revealing it. The gap between hint and revelation compels continued reading. Test hooks by asking whether someone could scroll past without needing to know more.

Assumption challenges work by contradicting common beliefs. "Posting more frequently kills your engagement" surprises readers expecting the opposite advice. "Hashtags are hurting your reach in 2026" contradicts conventional wisdom. Readers stop to understand why their assumptions might be wrong.

This technique requires genuine contrarian insight rather than manufactured controversy. Challenging assumptions you can't support damages credibility. The best assumption challenges come from real experience that revealed something unexpected.

Specific value promises work by stating exactly what readers will gain. "Five headline formulas that doubled my click rates" tells readers precisely what they get. "The exact script I use to turn replies into clients" promises actionable takeaway. Vague promises like "Great marketing tips" get ignored because they could mean anything.

The specificity matters enormously. Numbers create credibility. Exact implies reproducible rather than theoretical. Results framed in reader benefit rather than author accomplishment connect better.

Avoid hooks that work against you. Starting with "I" puts focus on yourself rather than reader benefit. Questions that can be answered yes or no get scrolled past because readers answer mentally and move on without engaging. Hooks longer than two lines lose readers before the message lands. Apologetic openings like "I know this is long but" signal low confidence and permission to skip.

Track hook performance by comparing first line patterns across your posts. Which opening structures correlate with higher impressions and engagement? Double down on patterns that work and abandon those that don't.

Thread Structure That Sustains Attention

Threads let you share longer thinking that single posts can't contain. But thread writing differs from single post writing in important ways. Each tweet must work independently while contributing to the larger argument. Readers can enter at any point or leave at any point.

The first tweet is your hook. It must work as a standalone post because most people will only see the first tweet in their feed. The For You algorithm surfaces individual tweets, not entire threads. If the hook fails, the thread dies before anyone sees your actual content.

Apply all hook principles to your opening tweet. Create curiosity, challenge assumptions, or promise specific value. Avoid opening with "Thread:" or similar labels that signal work ahead without promising reward.

Subsequent tweets should each contain one complete idea. Readers lose patience with tweets that trail off or require the next tweet to make sense. Every tweet should feel complete while also flowing into the next. The test: if someone saw only tweet four, would it make sense on its own?

Use numbers and structure to orient readers. "Thread on pricing strategy (7 tweets)" tells readers what to expect and how much time to invest. Some will appreciate this signaling and commit. Numbered points within the thread help readers track progress and enable easy reference to specific sections later.

End with clear takeaway and call to action. Summarize the main insight in the final tweet so readers who skimmed can catch the core message. Ask a question that invites replies. Suggest readers repost if they found value. Tell them what to do next. Threads that trail off without clear ending feel incomplete and generate less engagement.

Thread length should match content requirements rather than arbitrary targets. Short threads of 3 to 5 tweets work for focused insights that need more space than one tweet but don't warrant extensive treatment. Medium threads of 7 to 10 tweets handle frameworks and processes effectively. Long threads above 10 tweets risk losing readers and should be reserved for comprehensive guides that readers will bookmark for reference.

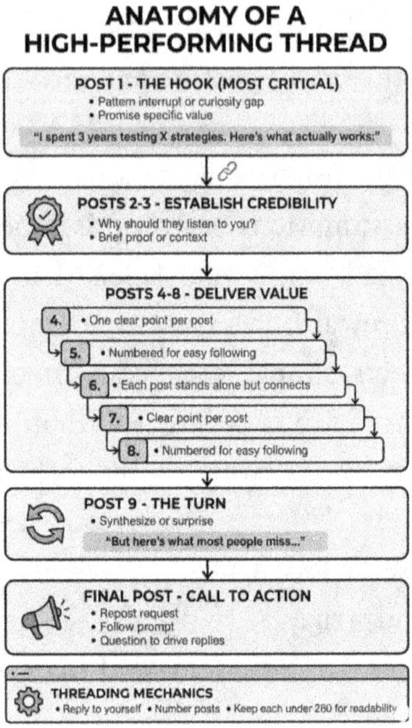

Figure 5.1: Anatomy of a High-Performing Thread

Thread Structures That Work

Certain thread structures reliably outperform others. Understanding these patterns helps you structure threads for maximum engagement.

The Framework Thread presents a mental model or process. Open with the problem the framework solves. Present the framework elements one per tweet. Close with implementation guidance. Example structure: "Most pricing strategies fail for one reason. Here's the framework that fixed pricing for 40+ clients. (Thread)" followed by framework elements.

The Contrarian Thread challenges conventional wisdom. Open with the belief you're challenging. Present evidence or rea soning against it. Offer alternative perspective. Address obvious objections. Close with nuanced conclusion. This structure generates engagement because people want to agree or disagree.

The Story Thread narrates a journey with lessons. Open with compelling situation or outcome. Walk through the story chronologically. Embed lessons within the narrative. Close with synthesized takeaways. Stories are memorable in ways that pure information isn't.

The Tactical Thread teaches specific implementation. Open with what readers will learn to do. Walk through steps sequentially. Include specific details that enable action. Close with expected results. Tactical threads get bookmarked and shared because they provide clear value.

The Listicle Thread compiles related items. Open with category and count. Present items one per tweet. Close with synthesis or reader prompt for additions. Listicles invite engagement through additions and disagreements.

Hook Formulas Reference

When struggling with hooks, use these templates as starting points:

Curiosity Gap: "I [unexpected action/result] before I learned [hint at lesson]."

Number Promise: "[Number] [specific outcome] that [transformed/fixed/changed] my [relevant area]."

Contrarian Setup: "[Common belief] is wrong. Here's why."

Story Tease: "In [year/situation], I made a decision that [consequence]. Here's what happened."

Direct Value: "The exact [asset] I use to [desirable outcome]."

Transformation: "I went from [bad state] to [good state] in [timeframe]. Here's how."

Question Flip: "Everyone asks how to [common question]. The real question is [better question]."

Warning: "The [common practice] that's killing your [area of concern]."

Customize these templates for your context. Generic hooks underperform hooks tailored to your specific expertise and audience.

Language That Drives Replies

Posts generating replies perform better than posts generating only likes. Replies signal genuine engagement. The algorithm rewards reply generating content with broader distribution because replies indicate the content sparked something worth responding to.

Questions invite responses when they're specific enough to answer easily but interesting enough to warrant response. The balance matters. "What is your biggest marketing challenge?" is too broad. The question could generate hundreds of different answers and none feel particularly called for. "What is the one tool you couldn't run your business without?" is specific and answerable. Readers know immediately whether they want to respond and what their response would be.

Opinions generate replies when they stake clear positions. "Hot take: SEO is dead for small businesses" invites agreement, disagreement, and debate. Neutral statements generating no disagreement also generate no engagement. The most engaging content takes stands rather than presenting both sides equally.

This doesn't mean manufacturing controversy. It means having actual perspectives based on experience and sharing them clearly.

Wishy washy content that hedges everything generates polite scrolling rather than engagement.

Lists inviting additions generate replies naturally. "Three books that changed how I think about pricing" invites others to share their recommendations. "My morning routine" invites others to share theirs. The content becomes conversation starter rather than broadcast.

Vulnerability generates replies when authentic. Sharing failures, challenges, or uncertainties invites support and shared experience. "I lost my biggest client this month. Here is what I learned." generates empathy and encouragement. But manufactured vulnerability feels manipulative and backfires. Audiences detect inauthenticity quickly.

Putting This Into Practice

A consultant had been posting detailed insights for six months with minimal engagement. Her content was genuinely valuable but her hooks were weak. Posts opened with "Here's something I've been thinking about lately" or "Wanted to share some thoughts on marketing strategy" followed by genuinely useful content that nobody saw.

She rewrote her hook approach using curiosity gaps and specific value promises. Same insights, different packaging. "I lost my biggest client by making this mistake" opened a post about project scoping issues. "The exact email template that books 80 percent of my discovery calls" opened a post about outreach strategy.

The target: significant impression growth within 30 days. The content had not changed. The hooks made it visible.

A freelance designer struggled with threads falling flat after strong starts. Opening tweets performed well but engagement dropped off by tweet three or four. Analysis revealed her subsequent tweets were not self-contained. Each required reading the previous tweet to make sense, and readers who jumped in mid-thread got confused and left.

She restructured threads so each tweet stood alone while contributing to the larger argument. Tweet three could make sense to someone who missed tweets one and two. Engagement on threads increased significantly, with replies distributed throughout rather than clustered only on the first tweet.

| 6 |

Using Multimedia on X

Inside This Chapter

We examine how images, videos, and other visual content perform differently than text on X. The analysis covers technical specifications ensuring quality display, strategic use cases for different formats, and the trade-offs between production quality and posting frequency that every creator must handle.

Video content drives significantly higher engagement than static text posts, with the algorithm prioritizing media that generates dwell time where users pause their scrolling. Visual content consistently outperforms text alone in reach and engagement metrics. Yet most business accounts post primarily text, leaving visual engagement advantages untapped. This chapter explains when and how to use multimedia strategically.

When Video Makes Sense

Video works best for demonstrations, personality, and complex explanations. Product walk-throughs showing software in action communicate more effectively than written descriptions ever could. Personal videos build connection that text can't replicate because audiences see facial expressions, hear tone, and feel human presence. Explanations requiring visual context benefit from screen recordings or whiteboard style presentations.

Video works poorly when text suffices. Simple announcements don't need video production. Tips that fit in a single sentence shouldn't become 60 second productions that waste viewer time and creator effort. Overproducing simple content feels excessive and may signal misunderstanding of the medium.

Technical requirements matter for quality display. X supports videos with varying length limits depending on account type. Optimal resolution is 1280 by 720 pixels minimum for clear display. File size limits apply. Vertical video performs well on mobile where most X consumption happens, though horizontal still works for desktop viewers.

Production quality matters less than authenticity in most cases. Polished corporate videos with multiple camera angles and professional editing often underperform rough smartphone clips that feel genuine and immediate. Talking head videos shot on phone in natural lighting typically outperform expensive productions because they feel real rather than manufactured.

This isn't permission to create unwatchable content. Audio quality matters more than video quality in viewer retention. Lighting should illuminate your face clearly. Background shouldn't distract. But perfectionism that prevents posting hurts more than imperfect videos that connect.

Short videos outperform long ones consistently. Attention spans on social feeds are brief. Videos under 60 seconds see significantly higher completion rates than longer content. Get to the point fast. If your video requires two minutes to deliver value, ensure the first 15 seconds promise that value clearly enough to earn the watch time.

Track video completion rates in X Analytics to understand where viewers drop off. If most viewers leave at the 20 second mark, your openings need work. If completion rates are strong but engagement is low, your call to action at the end needs improvement.

Video Content Types for Business

Different video formats serve different strategic purposes. Understanding the options helps you choose formats matched to your goals and production capacity.

Talking head videos show you speaking directly to camera. These build personal connection and establish your presence. Production requirements are minimal: phone camera, decent lighting, reasonable audio. Authenticity typically outweighs production value. Best for opinions, insights, and personal perspectives.

Screen recordings capture your screen while you narrate. These work well for demonstrations, tutorials, and walkthroughs. Use for software demonstrations, process explanations, and how-to content. Tools like Loom, QuickTime, or built-in screen recording make production simple.

Interview clips feature conversations with others. These require more coordination but provide variety and potentially access to others' audiences. Can be extracted from podcasts, webinars, or dedicated recording sessions. Best for expert positioning and relationship building.

Animation and motion graphics communicate concepts visually. Higher production requirements typically involving specialized tools or services. Best for explaining complex concepts, data visualization, and brand content. Not necessary for most accounts but differentiating when done well.

Text overlay videos show text appearing over static or simple moving backgrounds. Tools like Canva enable quick creation without filming. Work well for quote content, tips, and list-style content. Quick to produce once you establish a template.

Audio Quality Matters More Than Video

Counterintuitively, audio quality has greater impact on viewer retention than video quality. Viewers tolerate mediocre video more readily than they tolerate poor audio.

Built-in microphones on phones and laptops pick up room echo, background noise, and position themselves far from your mouth. Results are usable but noticeably amateur.

Lavalier microphones clipping to clothing dramatically improve audio quality for modest investment. USB options connecting directly to computers work for desk recording. Wireless options enable movement while filming.

Room acoustics affect results regardless of microphone quality. Hard surfaces reflect sound creating echo. Soft furnishings absorb sound creating cleaner audio. Recording in a room with carpet, curtains, and furniture typically sounds better than empty rooms with hard floors and bare walls.

Post-processing through simple tools can reduce background noise and normalize volume. Free tools like Audacity handle basic audio cleanup. Built-in options in video editing software often include noise reduction.

Image Creation for Non-Designers

You don't need design skills to create effective images for X. Template-based tools and simple approaches produce professional results.

Canva offers free and paid tiers with extensive template libraries. Templates for social media posts include proper sizing and design principles. Customize templates by changing colors, fonts, and text to match your brand. The free tier handles most needs.

Screenshots require zero design skill but provide high credibility. Actual results from analytics dashboards, customer testimonials captured as images, revenue numbers from your stripe dashboard. Real data carries more weight than designed graphics.

Simple photo editing through built-in phone tools or free apps like Snapseed handles basic improvements: cropping, brightness adjustment, basic filters. You don't need Photoshop for effective X images.

Branded templates you create once and reuse provide consistency without ongoing design effort. Create a template for quote graphics, tip graphics, and announcement graphics. Reuse the same layouts with different content.

Stock photos from Unsplash, Pexels, or other free sources provide professional imagery without production requirements. Choose images relevant to your content rather than generic business imagery. Add text overlay to stock photos using Canva for quick custom graphics.

When Images Work Best

Images stop scrolling more effectively than text alone while requiring less production effort than video. They represent the middle ground between text efficiency and video engagement.

Screenshots of data, results, or conversations add credibility to claims. Showing actual analytics dashboards proves performance claims. Customer testimonials captured as screenshots feel more authentic than retyped quotes. Revenue numbers displayed visually carry more weight than numbers typed in text. Always redact sensitive information and obtain permission before sharing client data or private metrics.

Infographics condense complex information into scannable format. Frameworks, processes, and comparisons work well as visual diagrams. The constraint of visual format forces clarity that verbose text explanations often lack.

Behind the scenes photos humanize brands and individuals. Office shots, work in progress images, and candid moments build connection by showing the human reality behind polished public presence.

Image specifications matter for quality display. Minimum 600 by 335 pixels for proper inline display without blurring or pixelation. Maximum file size 5 MB for photos. PNG format preserves sharp edges for graphics with text. JPEG format compresses photographic backgrounds better.

Multiple images in a single post create gallery experience. X displays up to four images in grid format. This works well for before and after comparisons, step by step process documentation, or multiple related examples that benefit from side by side viewing.

Animated Content and GIFs

GIFs communicate personality and humor efficiently. They work well for reactions to news or situations, celebrations of wins and milestones, and adding visual interest to announcements that would otherwise feel flat. X's native GIF library makes selection easy during post composition.

Use GIFs sparingly. Overuse feels unprofessional and may signal lack of substantive content. One GIF in a thread to break up text works. Occasional GIF replies to add personality work. Every post containing a GIF gets exhausting and undermines credibility.

Custom graphics and simple animations differentiate your content from accounts using only text or stock imagery. Canva and similar tools enable creation of branded graphics without design expertise. Consistent visual style across posts builds recognition, so audiences know your content before reading your name.

Putting This Into Practice

A bakery owner had posted exclusively text for a year with modest results. Engagement was acceptable but not growing. She started incorporating behind the scenes videos of bread baking, decorating cakes, and morning prep routines. Thirty second smartphone clips shot during normal work without special setup or editing.

Engagement increased 340 percent within 60 days. Video posts averaged 4,200 impressions compared to 900 for text posts using the same account. More importantly, foot traffic increased 23 percent with new customers specifically mentioning the videos when asked how they discovered the bakery. The visual content communicated artisan-ship and care that text descriptions couldn't match.

The lesson was not that video always wins, but that video showcasing visual craft resonates in ways text can't replicate. A bakery has visual appeal worth showing. An accounting firm might find different results.

A consultant found the opposite lesson through over investment in video production. He started creating elaborate video content requiring hours of production per post: scripting, multiple takes, editing, thumbnail design. While individual videos performed well when published, his posting frequency dropped from daily to twice weekly because production consumed available time.

Total engagement actually decreased because fewer posts meant fewer total impressions and touch-points with audience. The polished videos couldn't compensate for reduced presence.

He shifted to mixing formats strategically. Twice weekly video content with meaningful production value for topics warranting visual treatment. Daily text posts and occasional image posts requiring minimal production for ideas that did not need video. This balanced quality video content with consistent presence, optimizing for total impact rather than per-post perfection.

| 7 |

Scheduling, Tools, & Workflow

Inside This Chapter

We examine scheduling tools and how they transform content creation from daily scrambling into systematic workflow. The analysis covers tool selection criteria matched to different business contexts, batching systems that create content banks rather than rigid calendars, and hybrid approaches balancing automated consistency with reactive engagement.

You schedule posts every Sunday for the coming week. Seven posts drafted, seven optimal times selected, seven publications queued. By Wednesday morning, three scheduled posts feel irrelevant because industry news broke Tuesday afternoon. Your carefully planned content about quarterly marketing trends looks tone deaf when everyone discusses the major platform algorithm change announced 18 hours ago.

The problem isn't scheduling tools failing but treating scheduling as set and forget automation rather than dynamic workflow supporting both consistency and flexibility. This chapter teaches tool selection and workflow design that enables scheduled consistency without sacrificing relevance.

How Scheduling Tools Help

Marketers using automated scheduling report 65 percent improved posting frequency after implementation. Scheduling eliminates the burden of remembering to post daily while maintaining consistent audience presence. This reliability matters especially for small teams managing multiple platforms where daily manual posting across channels becomes unsustainable.

Native X scheduling provides basic functionality, letting you schedule posts up to 18 months in advance. Click the calendar icon when composing a post, select date and time, and the post queues automatically. However, native scheduling limits you to scheduling one post at a time without bulk upload capabilities. For accounts posting frequently, entering each post individually becomes impractical and time consuming.

Third party tools offer advanced capabilities justifying their cost for many accounts. Bulk CSV scheduling uploads dozens or hundreds of posts simultaneously from a spreadsheet. Cross platform posting manages X, LinkedIn, Instagram, and Facebook from a single dashboard rather than logging into each platform separately. Team collaboration features enable approval workflows where one person drafts and another reviews before publication. Visual calendars let you see your entire content plan at a glance and drag posts to reschedule as needed.

The question is whether tool costs justify time savings for your specific situation. Calculate your ROI during free trial periods that most platforms offer. Track time spent scheduling with the tool compared to previous manual posting. If monthly time value saved exceeds tool cost, the subscription pays for itself. If not, native scheduling may suffice for your posting volume.

Choosing the Right Tool

Different workflows require different tool capabilities. Solo creators posting primarily to X need basic scheduling with calendar view for planning, mobile app for adjustments while away from desk, and simple analytics showing what performs. These features enable core scheduling workflow without complexity that slows down individual creator workflows.

Buffer serves budget conscious users testing scheduling before premium investment. The free tier covers three channels with basic scheduling. The interface is simple and reliable without overwhelming feature lists. Best for individuals starting their scheduling journey who want to validate the approach before paying.

SocialBee serves solo creators and small businesses wanting automation with content variety. Content categories cycle through different post types automatically, ensuring pillar balance without manual tracking. Evergreen content republishes at intervals you define, extending the life of proven posts. Pricing starts at $29 monthly with 14 day free trial. Best for accounts wanting consistent presence without daily attention.

Hootsuite and Sprout Social serve agencies and larger teams needing enterprise features. Advanced analytics across accounts, team permissions controlling who can post versus who can only draft, and client management separating different businesses cleanly. These features justify higher costs for organizations managing multiple accounts professionally but represent overkill for solo creators.

Test before committing. Most platforms offer 14 day trials. Schedule one complete week of content during trial, testing bulk upload if you plan to batch create, calendar usability for planning and rescheduling, preview accuracy to ensure posts display as intended, and mobile app functionality for on the go adjustments. Focus evaluation on features matching your actual workflow rather than impressive capability lists you will never use.

The 70/30 Hybrid Model

Schedule 70 percent of content in advance. Reserve 30 percent capacity for reactive engagement with trending topics and conversations that couldn't be predicted.

This balance enables both consistency and authenticity. Scheduled content maintains baseline presence even when you're busy with client work, traveling, or dealing with personal matters. Reserved capacity lets you participate in timely discussions when opportunities arise without feeling locked into an inflexible calendar.

Track your scheduled versus reactive ratio monthly. Count posts from your scheduling tool versus posts created in the moment. If scheduled content exceeds 90 percent, your presence may feel robotic and you're missing trending opportunities that could expand reach. If reactive content exceeds 50 percent, your strategy lacks structure and you're probably scrambling unnecessarily.

Posting consistency above 90 percent matters more than posting frequency for audience trust and algorithmic favor. Better to schedule three posts weekly and hit them reliably than schedule seven posts and miss half due to overcommitment. The algorithm rewards accounts that show up consistently more than accounts that post heavily in bursts.

Batching Systems

Weekly batching dedicates 90 minutes every Sunday or Monday to draft 10 to 15 posts for the coming week. This approach keeps content timely because you're only looking one week ahead and can respond to recent developments in your drafts. However, missing one session immediately creates a content gap the following week with no buffer.

Monthly batching dedicates three hours once monthly to generate content for the entire month ahead. This approach provides substantial buffer against busy periods and reduces total batching sessions from 52 yearly to 12. However, content created a month ago may feel dated by publication if your industry moves quickly or if developments change relevance.

Choose based on your working style and schedule reliability. Weekly batching suits creators who think topically and generate ideas from current conversations they observed that week. Monthly batching suits those who plan strategically and think in campaigns or themes that remain relevant over longer periods.

Either approach beats daily scrambling. The discipline of dedicated batching sessions creates content banks ensuring you always have material ready regardless of daily pressures. When you have 20 drafted posts waiting, missing a single day of creation doesn't create crisis.

Tool Selection Decision Framework

Choosing scheduling tools overwhelms many users. This framework simplifies the decision based on your actual needs.

First, define your requirements honestly. Answer these questions: How many social platforms do you actively manage? How many posts per week do you create? Do you work solo or with a team? What is your monthly budget for tools? Which features are essential versus nice-to-have?

Solo creators managing one to two platforms: Native scheduling or Buffer free tier handles basic needs. Upgrade to paid tools only if specific features justify cost. Essential features: visual calendar, mobile app, basic analytics. Nice-to-have features: bulk upload, AI suggestions.

Small teams managing two to four platforms: Consider tools with collaboration features. Buffer paid, Later, or similar mid-tier tools provide needed capability without enterprise complexity. Essential features: team access, approval workflows, cross-platform posting. Nice-to-have features: content library, advanced analytics.

Agencies managing five or more accounts: Enterprise tools like Sprout Social, Hootsuite Business, or Agorapulse handle scale and client separation. Essential features: client management, white-label reporting, team permissions. Investment justified by efficiency at scale.

Don't over-buy. Tools with features you will never use represent wasted budget. Start simpler than you think you need. Upgrade when specific limitations become painful rather than anticipating needs that may not materialize.

Workflow Optimization Techniques

Beyond basic batching, these techniques optimize your content workflow.

Template creation reduces repetitive decisions. Create post templates for common content types: tip format, question format, case study format. Templates speed drafting by providing structure. Store templates in your content bank document for easy access.

Asset organization prevents time lost searching. Create folder structure for images, graphics, and other visual assets. Use consistent naming conventions. Maintain a brand asset folder with logos, colors, and approved imagery.

Scheduling time blocking dedicates specific times to specific activities. Rather than mixing creation, scheduling, and engagement throughout the day, block dedicated time for each. Creation requires creative energy best deployed during peak focus. Scheduling is administrative and can happen during lower energy periods. Engagement requires responsiveness and fits between other activities.

Capture systems prevent lost ideas. Ideas occur at random times. Without capture systems, ideas disappear before batching sessions. Use your phone's notes app, voice memos, or dedicated tool to capture ideas immediately when they occur. Review captures during batching sessions.

Putting This Into Practice

A marketing agency tripled client capacity after implementing systematic scheduling workflows. Before systematization, one account manager handled 4 clients with constant stress. Manual posting for each client consumed 15 hours weekly. Quality suffered as volume pressure forced rushed content.

They implemented monthly batching with scheduling tool deployment. Three hour monthly sessions per client generated 60 to 80 posts covering 70 percent of posting needs. Scheduled content maintained presence automatically. Reserved capacity enabled timely responses to industry news relevant to each client.

The same account manager now handles 12 clients while working 42 hours weekly instead of 55. Client retention improved from 75 percent annually to 92 percent as consistency increased and last minute scrambling decreased. The efficiency gain came not from working harder but from working systematically.

A nonprofit communications director maintained presence through a major organizational crisis using batched content. When an emergency demanded full attention for three weeks, including leadership transition and urgent donor communications, she had no time for X content creation. Scheduled posts continued publishing automatically, maintaining audience connection. Engagement remained stable because presence continued even without active management.

When the crisis resolved, she resumed normal workflow without rebuilding lost momentum. The batched content buffer absorbed disruption that would have silenced accounts without such systems.

| 8 |

Understanding the X Algorithm

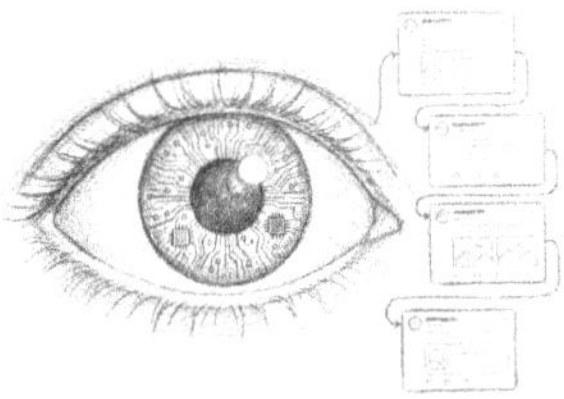

Inside This Chapter

We examine how the X algorithm decides which posts get seen and which disappear. The analysis covers ranking factors that determine distribution, engagement signals the algorithm prioritizes, and strategic approaches to working with algorithmic distribution rather than fighting against it.

You post something you consider genuinely valuable. It gets 200 impressions. Your competitor posts something similar, maybe even less insightful. It gets 20,000 impressions. The difference isn't content quality or timing alone. It is understanding how the algorithm evaluates and distributes content.

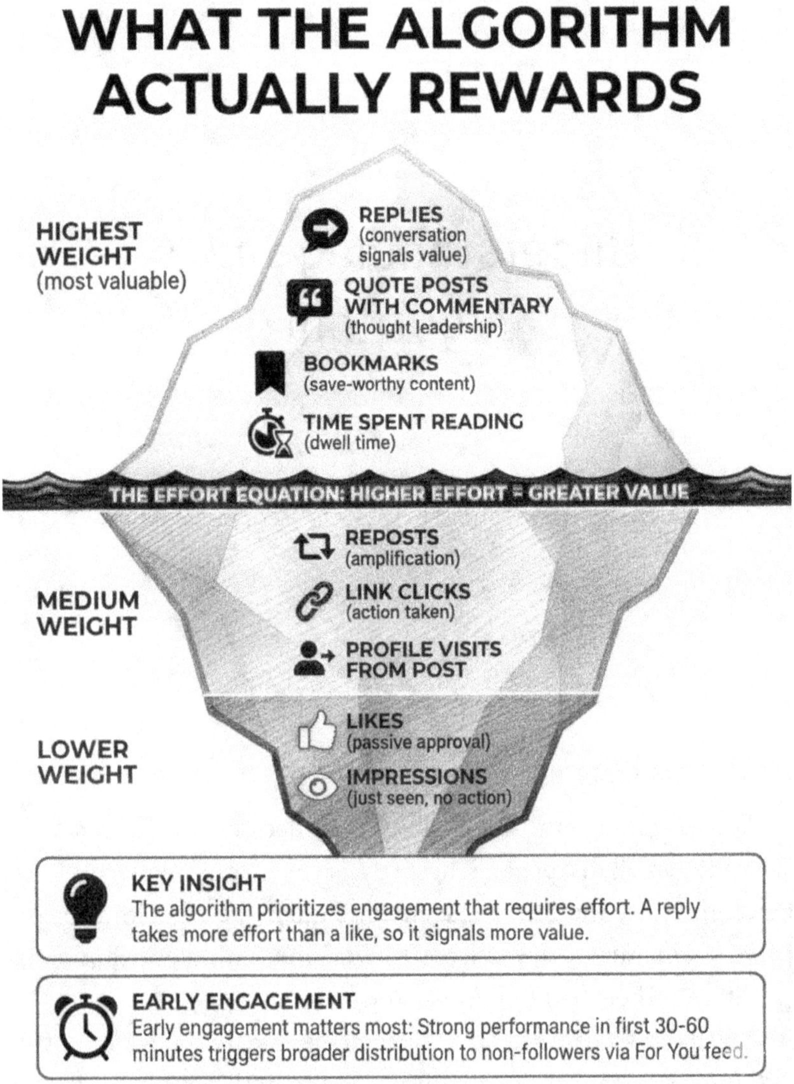

Figure 8.1: What the Algorithm Actually Rewards

How the Algorithm Works

The X algorithm evaluates every post against hundreds of signals to determine who sees it and how broadly it distributes. Understanding the primary signals helps you create content the algorithm promotes rather than suppresses.

Engagement velocity matters enormously and represents one of the strongest signals. Posts generating likes, replies, and reposts quickly after publication get distributed more broadly. The algorithm interprets early engagement as quality signal because humans found it worth interacting with immediately. Posts with slow initial engagement get limited distribution regardless of eventual performance. The algorithm makes distribution decisions within the first hour or two.

The tactical application is clear: post when your audience is active so early engagement can accumulate. Check your analytics for peak activity times when your specific followers are online. Schedule important content for those windows. The same content posted at 3 AM when your audience sleeps versus 10 AM when they scroll during coffee break will perform dramatically differently.

Replies carry more weight than likes. The algorithm treats replies as stronger engagement signals because they require more effort than tapping a heart icon. Writing a response indicates genuine investment. Posts generating conversations get promoted over posts generating passive approval.

This means content designed to spark replies outperforms content optimized for likes. Questions, opinions, and incomplete thoughts that invite completion generate more algorithmic reward than polished broadcasts that require no response.

Account authority affects distribution in ways that favor established accounts. Accounts with consistent posting history, strong engagement rates, and established follower relationships get wider initial distribution than new or inconsistent accounts. This authority builds over time through sustained activity.

The implication for new accounts: early growth is hard not because your content is bad but because you haven't yet built algorithmic authority. Consistency over months builds this authority gradually. No shortcut.

Content type influences reach in predictable patterns. Video content receives algorithmic boost because the platform wants to compete with TikTok and YouTube. Threads get promoted when early tweets perform well because threads keep users on platform longer. Images outperform plain text. The algorithm rewards content formats that keep users engaged with X rather than leaving to consume content elsewhere.

Time spent on post matters independently of engagement. Posts where users pause and read rather than scroll past signal quality. Longer dwell time leads to broader distribution. This makes hooks so critical. Stopping the scroll creates the dwell time that triggers algorithmic promotion even before engagement accumulates.

Working With the Algorithm

Post when your audience is active. Engagement velocity depends on reaching people who will engage immediately during the critical early window. Check your X Analytics for when your specific followers are most active. These patterns vary by audience type: B2B audiences peak during business hours while consumer audiences may peak evenings and weekends.

Respond to early engagement quickly. When someone replies to your post in the first hour, reply back promptly. This back and forth signals active conversation happening, which triggers broader distribution. The algorithm sees discussion occurring and shares it with more people who might join.

Create content inviting replies rather than passive consumption. Questions, opinions, and incomplete thoughts generate more algorithmic reward than polished statements that require no response. "What is your unpopular marketing opinion?" generates more algorithmic benefit than "Here are five marketing tips."

Maintain posting consistency. Sporadic posting damages algorithmic standing because the platform can't reliably predict your activity. Regular activity signals active account worth promoting. Even during slow periods, maintain minimum posting frequency to preserve algorithmic authority.

Avoid engagement bait that backfires. Explicitly asking people to retweet, using excessive hashtags, or posting identical content repeatedly can trigger spam signals. The algorithm punishes obvious manipulation. Earned engagement from quality content outperforms requested engagement from begging.

Algorithmic Signals Ranked

Understanding signal strength helps prioritize tactics. The algorithm weights signals differently based on the effort and intent they represent.

Strongest positive signals: Replies with substantive content indicating genuine engagement. Extended dwell time showing users read rather than scrolled past. Quote posts with commentary showing enough value to warrant sharing with added perspective. Profile visits following post view indicating curiosity about the author.

Moderate positive signals: Reposts without commentary showing approval but less investment than quote posts. Likes indicating mild positive response. Link clicks showing willingness to leave platform for your content. Follows from post viewers representing commitment to future content.

Weak positive signals: Brief dwell time showing the post stopped scroll momentarily. Bookmarks for later reading. Views without engagement indicating content was seen but did not compel action.

Negative signals that damage distribution: Users hiding your posts indicating they don't want to see similar content. Unfollows after viewing posts indicating content drove them away. Muting indicating persistent annoyance. Reports indicating policy concerns or severe quality problems.

The practical implication: optimize for replies and quote posts rather than likes. Create content people want to discuss, not just approve of.

Timing Strategy Details

Optimal timing varies by audience type, but patterns exist worth understanding.

B2B audiences peak during business hours in their time zones. Morning scrolling while having coffee, lunch break browsing, and late afternoon wind-down represent common engagement windows. Weekends typically see significant engagement drops for B2B content.

Consumer audiences peak evenings and weekends when people have leisure time. Late night scrolling before bed represents a significant engagement window for entertainment and lifestyle content.

Global audiences require multiple posting times to reach different time zones. If you serve audiences across US, Europe, and Asia, no single posting time reaches all audiences during peak hours. Consider alternating posting times to reach different geographic segments.

Your specific audience may differ from general patterns. Use X Analytics to identify when your followers are most active rather than relying on generic guidance. Test different posting times with similar content to identify your optimal windows empirically.

Engagement Types Ranked

Not all engagement is equal. The algorithm weights different interaction types differently.

Replies with substantive content rank highest. Someone writing a thoughtful response indicates genuine value worth distributing to others who might respond similarly. Quote tweets with commentary rank second. Sharing while adding perspective signals content worth amplifying beyond simple agreement. Reposts without commentary rank third. Simple amplification indicates approval but less strongly than added perspective. Likes rank lowest among positive signals. Easy to give, likes indicate mild approval but limited engagement depth.

Negative signals also affect distribution. Users hiding your posts, unfollowing after seeing your content, or reporting posts signals quality problems. The algorithm reduces distribution for accounts generating negative responses. If your content causes people to unfollow or hide, you will see reduced reach even on content that doesn't generate these reactions.

Build strategy around generating high value engagement. Create content worth replying to. Ask questions worth answering. Share perspectives worth debating. Optimize for conversation rather than vanity metrics that look good but don't signal value to the algorithm.

Putting This Into Practice

A local coffee roaster had decent content but minimal reach. Posts about specialty coffee techniques that deserved audience received only 300 to 500 impressions consistently. Analysis revealed posting at random times whenever inspiration struck, often late evening when her target audience of local coffee enthusiasts was not active. Early engagement was always slow because posts published when followers were sleeping or busy.

She analyzed her X Analytics and identified peak engagement windows when her specific followers were most active. Posts shifted to those times: 7:30 AM when people scrolled during morning coffee and 12:30 PM during lunch breaks. Engagement velocity increased immediately because more followers saw content during the critical early window.

The same content with better timing generated 3x the impressions. Nothing changed about what she wrote or how she wrote it. The algorithm simply had more early engagement signals to work with.

A consultant escaped a reach plateau by changing content strategy rather than posting time. He had been posting polished insights optimized for appreciation and likes. Reach had flatlined for months despite consistent effort because likes don't trigger distribution as strongly as replies.

He shifted to posting opinions and questions inviting responses. Instead of "Here's how to write better proposals in five steps" he posted "Unpopular opinion: Most proposal templates actually hurt your close rate. Here's why." The controversial framing invited replies from people who agreed, disagreed, or wanted elaboration. The algorithm saw conversation happening and distributed the content more broadly.

Within 60 days, average impressions per post doubled. Follower growth accelerated from 50 weekly to 200 weekly. The content quality had not changed. What changed was consistency and timing, which allowed the algorithm to recognize the account as reliably active. Research from IIDE confirms this pattern: reach amplification follows consistent posting and engagement more than content quality improvements.

| 9 |

Hashtags, Tags, & Visibility Tactics

Inside This Chapter

We examine hashtags, mentions, and other visibility tactics on X. The analysis covers when hashtags help versus hurt reach based on current platform dynamics, strategic tagging of other accounts without being annoying, and visibility approaches beyond basic tactics.

Conventional wisdom says use hashtags for discovery. Conventional wisdom is increasingly wrong. The relationship between hashtags and reach has changed significantly as the platform evolved. What worked in 2015 often hurts performance in 2026. This chapter separates current reality from outdated advice.

The Current State of Hashtags

Hashtags on X now function differently than most users assume based on old guidance. Excessive hashtags correlate with reduced engagement rather than increased discovery. Posts with 1 to 2 relevant hashtags often outperform posts with 5 or more hashtags.

The algorithm treats hashtag stuffing as spam signal. Posts crammed with hashtags get suppressed rather than promoted because the behavior pattern matches spam accounts. The practice that once drove discovery now often limits it.

Hashtag search has also declined in user behavior. Most discovery now happens through algorithmic feeds rather than hashtag browsing. Users scrolling For You pages encounter content the algorithm promotes based on engagement signals, not content tagged with specific hashtags they searched. The discovery mechanism has shifted away from hashtags toward algorithmic curation.

This doesn't mean hashtags are useless. Strategic hashtag use still helps in specific contexts where active hashtag communities exist. Industry conversations often coalesce around specific hashtags during events or campaigns. Niche communities maintain active hashtag use for topic organization. Breaking news and live events still benefit from relevant hashtags as users search to follow developing stories.

The guidance is to use hashtags sparingly and strategically rather than automatically adding them to every post hoping for discovery.

When Hashtags Help

Event participation benefits significantly from hashtags. Conference hashtags, live event tags, and campaign hashtags create discoverable participation in ongoing conversations. If you're attending an industry conference with an official hashtag, using that tag connects your content to the conversation where interested people are actively looking.

Niche community engagement benefits when those communities actively use specific hashtags. Some professional communities organize around tags and browse them regularly. Research whether your target audience actually follows and uses specific hashtags before assuming they do. The only way to know is checking whether hashtag search surfaces active recent content from accounts your audience follows.

Trending topic participation benefits from using the trending hashtag when your content genuinely relates to the topic. Trending hashtags receive surge of attention as users explore what others are saying. However, forcing unrelated content into trending conversations through irrelevant hashtag use damages credibility and may trigger spam signals.

When Hashtags Hurt

Regular posts about general topics in your expertise area rarely benefit from hashtags. A post sharing business advice doesn't need hashtags appended. The algorithm will distribute it based on engagement signals from your followers and network, not hashtag presence.

Excessive hashtags consistently hurt performance across almost all account types. Posts with 5 or more hashtags typically see lower engagement than posts with 1 to 2 or none at all. The visual clutter alone reduces readability and signals desperation for attention.

Irrelevant hashtags damage credibility beyond hurting reach. Using popular but unrelated hashtags to chase visibility backfires because users who find your content through those hashtags immediately recognize the mismatch and may hide or report the content. The algorithm may flag it as spam behavior affecting future distribution.

Strategic Mentions and Tags

Mentioning other accounts strategically increases visibility when done authentically because tagging notifies the tagged account of your post. If a larger account engages with your mention, their audience may discover you through that interaction.

The key word is authentically. Tagging accounts hoping they will amplify your content without genuine relevance annoys people and damages potential relationships. Tag accounts when you're genuinely referencing their work, responding to something they said, including them in conversation they would naturally care about, or giving credit for ideas or inspiration.

Quote tweeting with added commentary works better than simple reposting for building relationships and visibility. Adding your perspective to someone else's content creates value and shows thought partnership. Simple reposting shows you saw something but doesn't show what you think about it.

Building relationships through consistent engagement over time generates more sustainable visibility than tactical tagging. Accounts that regularly engage with your content become natural amplifiers because they recognize and appreciate your presence. Trying to shortcut this through cold tagging rarely works and often annoys.

Conversation Participation Strategy

Beyond hashtags and mentions, strategic conversation participation expands reach through natural engagement.

Find relevant conversations: Use X search to find discussions about topics in your expertise area. Follow accounts that consistently start valuable conversations. Set up notifications for specific accounts whose discussions you want to join. Monitor trending topics for opportunities to contribute expertise.

Add value in replies: Generic agreement adds nothing. Specific insights, relevant examples, or thoughtful questions add value that reflects well on you. The goal: showing expertise, not getting attention through volume.

Time replies strategically: Early replies to high-profile posts get more visibility than late replies buried in long threads. Monitor accounts whose posts consistently generate engagement and reply early when they post. Premium Plus subscribers benefit most from this timing strategy due to reply prioritization.

Follow up on conversations: When your replies generate responses, continue the conversation. Building ongoing dialogue creates relationship beyond single interaction. The person you converse with may become follower, collaborator, or customer.

Quote Post Strategy

Quote posts with added commentary provide value that simple reposts can't match while expanding reach to your audience.

Commentary types that work: Adding your perspective on why the original content matters. Providing additional context the original lacks. Offering respectful disagreement with reasoning. Connecting the content to your expertise area. Asking questions the original content raises.

Commentary types that fail: Simply saying "This!" or "Great post!" which adds nothing. Hijacking the content to promote yourself without relevant connection. Disagreeing without reasoning or respectfully. Writing commentary longer than justified by the original content.

Attribution matters: Quote posts naturally attribute through the embedded original post. Also, acknowledging the original creator builds relationship. "Excellent point from @handle, this connects to something I've been thinking about..."

Strategic targeting: Quote post accounts whose audiences overlap with yours. The original creator's followers see your commentary and may discover you through it. Quote post content from accounts larger than yours to access their audience.

Putting This Into Practice

A consultant analyzed three months of her posting data and found an inverse correlation between hashtag use and engagement. Posts with no hashtags averaged 2,100 impressions. Posts with 3 or more hashtags averaged 1,400 impressions. The hashtags she had been adding religiously were not helping. They were actively hurting reach.

She eliminated routine hashtag use entirely, reserving hashtags only for live events and trending topics directly relevant to her expertise. Three months later, average impressions had increased 40 percent. Research by Rauschnabel (2019) demonstrates that hashtag motivations and effectiveness vary significantly by platform and user behavior patterns, with strategic application outperforming routine usage across different account types.

A nonprofit communications director took the opposite approach and found success through strategic hashtag use in specific contexts. She identified three industry hashtags with active communities: nonprofit practitioners who regularly searched and engaged with content using specific sector tags.

She used these hashtags only when participating in those specific conversations where the hashtag made sense contextually. General posts about her organization's work had no hashtags. Posts specifically engaging with sector-wide discussions used the relevant community tag.

Engagement on community hashtag posts significantly outperformed general posts, running nearly 3x higher. The hashtags worked in this context because they connected content to active community conversations rather than hoping for generic discovery from strangers browsing random tags.

| 10 |

Collaborations & Cross-Promotion

Inside This Chapter

We examine how partnerships accelerate growth beyond what solo effort can achieve. The analysis covers identifying strategic partners with appropriate audience overlap, approaching them professionally without seeming desperate, structuring partnerships for mutual benefit, and measuring whether collaborations deliver qualified growth rather than vanity metrics.

You post consistently. Your content quality is strong. Your engagement tactics work. Yet you reach the same few thousand people month after month while watching others with similar or weaker content achieve breakthrough growth. The difference often lies not in what they do alone but in who they partner with strategically. This chapter teaches partnership development from identification through execution to measurement.

Why Partnerships Matter

Solo organic growth operates linearly. You create content, some percentage of viewers engage, a fraction of engaged viewers follow, and growth accumulates gradually over time. Partnership growth operates exponentially. When you collaborate with an account reaching 10,000 followers, you potentially access all 10,000 immediately rather than building awareness one person at a time over months.

Effective collaborations generate three distinct value transfers. Audience transfer introduces you to followers of your partner who have never encountered your account. These people already trust content their followed accounts engage with, so the introduction carries implicit endorsement. Credibility transfer occurs when your partner's engagement signals trustworthiness to their audience. If an account they respect collaborates with you, you inherit some of that respect. Content multiplication happens when partnership content gets distributed across multiple channels simultaneously, achieving reach neither party could accomplish independently.

The quality of transferred audience matters more than quantity. Partnering with an account reaching 50,000 people with no interest in your work generates zero value despite impressive reach numbers. Followers gained from irrelevant partnerships unfollow quickly or never engage. Partnering with an account reaching 2,000 highly targeted people who match your ideal audience profile generates sustainable growth with engaged followers who actually care about your content.

The data supports this approach. Brands engaging in strategic collaborations achieve 3.2 times faster follower growth and 4.7 times higher engagement rates compared to brands relying solely on organic content. The effect is most pronounced for organizations with fewer than 10,000 followers breaking through initial visibility barriers where solo organic growth is slowest.

Finding the Right Partners

Optimal partnerships have 15 to 40 percent audience overlap. This range balances shared interest with new reach. Under 15 percent overlap signals insufficient shared interest, making content collaboration difficult because your audiences care about different things. The partnership feels forced. Over 40 percent overlap indicates excessive audience duplication, limiting new follower acquisition potential because most of your partner's followers already follow you.

Look for accounts serving adjacent rather than identical audiences. A business productivity app might partner with a student success account to reach younger professionals interested in productivity. A marketing consultant might partner with a web developer to offer integrated perspectives on digital business building. A local coffee shop might partner with a neighborhood bookstore sharing community-minded customers interested in local businesses.

Size matters but not in the way most assume. Partnering with accounts having 0.5 to 3 times your follower count works better than chasing massive accounts far beyond your size. Similar sized accounts have mutual incentive for collaboration because both benefit relatively equally. An account with 100,000 followers has little reason to partner with an account having 500 because the value exchange is dramatically unequal.

Values alignment prevents partnership damage that can take years to repair. Review potential partners' content thoroughly before proposing collaboration. Examine not just topics but tone, positions on industry issues, and professional behavior. Ensure their voice and conduct align with your brand. One poorly chosen partnership with an account that later becomes controversial can cost credibility that took years to build.

Approaching Potential Partners

Build authentic relationships before pitching partnerships. Engage genuinely with their content for 4 to 6 weeks before proposing anything formal. Comment thoughtfully on their posts with substance rather than generic praise. Share their content with added perspective showing you actually engaged with the ideas. Become familiar to them through consistent presence before asking for anything.

This relationship building matters enormously. Partnership proposal acceptance rates jump from under 10 percent with cold outreach to 25 to 35 percent when relationships exist first. The time invested in genuine engagement pays off in partnership success rates.

Partnership proposals should articulate mutual benefit explicitly. What specifically does the partner gain from collaborating with you? Access to your audience and their attention. Your expertise complementing theirs. Content creation capacity they might lack. Make the value exchange clear rather than assuming they will figure out why it benefits them.

Effective proposals are specific about what you're suggesting. A vague "we should collaborate sometime" gets ignored because it requires the recipient to do work imagining what collaboration might look like. A specific proposal like "I'd like to co-host an X

Space next month discussing productivity tools for remote teams, with you covering the technical evaluation criteria and me covering the workflow integration considerations" gives the partner something concrete to evaluate and respond to.

The Four-Stage Partnership Process

Successful partnerships follow a predictable development process rather than emerging from random opportunities. This systematic approach converts more initial contacts into productive relationships.

Stage One: Identification (Weeks 1 to 2). Research potential partners methodically rather than waiting for opportunities to appear. Identify 10 to 15 candidates meeting your criteria: appropriate audience overlap (15 to 40 percent), follower count within reasonable range of yours (0.5x to 3x), values alignment evident in their content, and complementary rather than competitive positioning. Document candidates in a tracking spreadsheet with notes on why each is promising.

Stage Two: Relationship Building (Weeks 3 to 6). Before proposing anything formal, build genuine relationship through engagement. Comment thoughtfully on their posts, adding value rather than generic praise. Share their content with your perspective added. Reply to their questions and discussions. Become a recognizable presence in their notifications. This investment pays off in proposal acceptance rates.

Stage Three: Proposal Development (Weeks 7 to 8). Craft specific proposals articulating mutual benefit clearly. Explain what you're proposing, what you bring to the partnership, and what they would gain. Be specific about format, timeline, and deliverables. Tailor proposals to each potential partner's specific situation rather than sending identical pitches.

Stage Four: Execution and Measurement (Weeks 9 onward). For accepted proposals, execute professionally and measure results rigorously. Track follower growth, engagement metrics, and business outcomes during partnership periods. Document lessons for future partnerships. Maintain relationship after initial collaboration for potential ongoing partnership.

Partnership Proposal Template

Effective proposals include specific elements that increase acceptance rates:

Opening: Reference your existing relationship. "I've enjoyed our exchanges about [topic] over the past few weeks..."

Value Proposition: State clearly what you're proposing and why it benefits them. "I'd like to propose a co-authored thread series where we each contribute expertise on [complementary topics]. Your audience would gain [specific value], and you'd reach my [audience size and description]."

Specifics: Detail the logistics. "I'm thinking a three-thread series published over consecutive Tuesdays in [month]. Each thread would be 8 to 10 tweets, with us alternating contributions. I'd handle coordination and scheduling."

Your Contribution: Be explicit about what you bring. "I'll contribute expertise on [your area], my audience of [size and description], and handle production logistics."

Ask: Clear request for response. "Would you be interested in exploring this? Happy to jump on a quick call or continue discussing here."

Follow-up: Timeline for response. "I'll follow up next week if I don't hear back, but no pressure if this isn't the right timing."

Measuring Partnership Success

Partnerships require measurement to determine whether they deliver value justifying the time investment.

Follower attribution during partnership: Track new followers gained during partnership periods compared to baseline growth rates. If you normally gain 100 followers weekly and gain 180 during partnership week, approximately 80 followers are attributable to partnership.

Follower quality assessment: Analyze profiles of partnership-attributed followers. Do they match your target audience? Are they likely to engage and eventually convert? High follower gains with poor quality attribution indicate audience fit problems.

Engagement lift on partnership content: Compare engagement rates on partnership content versus your typical content. Partnership content should generate 2x to 3x your normal engagement due to combined audiences and content novelty.

Business outcomes: Track leads, inquiries, and conversions during partnership periods. The ultimate test is whether partnerships generate business results beyond engagement metrics.

Partnership efficiency: Calculate time invested in partnership development and execution versus results generated. Some partnerships require extensive coordination for modest results. Others generate significant value with minimal effort. Learn which partnership types deliver efficiently for your situation.

Executing Collaborations Well

Co-created content outperforms simple cross-promotion by significant margins. Content where both partners contribute meaningfully creates value that neither could create alone. A thread where each partner contributes expertise on alternating tweets shows combined knowledge. An X Space featuring both perspectives creates conversation audiences can't get elsewhere. A case study showing how combined approaches solved problems shows practical partnership value.

Simple cross-promotion feels hollow and often annoys audiences. A post saying "Check out my partner @Account" provides no value to anyone's audience. It asks followers to invest attention without offering return. The content should show why the partnership exists and what audiences gain from it.

Coordinate timing so both partners' audiences see content during peak engagement windows. Schedule collaborative posts when both audiences are active so early engagement can accumulate from both communities. This coordination maximizes the combined reach benefit and shows both partners invested in success.

Partnership content should achieve 2 to 3 times your normal engagement rate due to combined audience activation and content novelty. If partnership content performs at or below your baseline, either the collaboration format is weak, failing to use both parties effectively, or the audience fit is poor and your followers don't care about your partner's expertise.

Putting This Into Practice

A marketing consultant had strong content but plateaued growth hovering around 3,500 followers for months. She identified five potential partners through systematic research: two agencies serving different client types than hers, a business coach with complementary focus on operations rather than marketing, a tech reviewer covering tools her clients used, and a podcast host in adjacent space discussing business building.

She spent six weeks engaging genuinely with each account before proposing anything. She replied thoughtfully to their threads.

She shared their content with added commentary showing she engaged with the ideas. She became a familiar presence in their notifications.

When she reached out with specific proposals, four of five responded positively, far exceeding typical cold outreach response rates. Three resulted in executed partnerships over the following quarter: co-authored threads combining her marketing expertise with their operational or technical perspectives, guest appearances on an X Space series the podcast host ran, and a joint case study with one agency showing how their combined services helped a shared client.

During the partnership quarter, her follower growth increased 67 percent compared to the previous quarter despite posting at similar frequency. More importantly, inquiry quality improved noticeably. Prospects mentioned seeing the partnerships and came pre-qualified because partners' endorsements established credibility before prospects ever visited her profile.

An e-commerce brand found the opposite lesson through poor partner selection. Excited by follower count, they partnered with a lifestyle influencer whose 85,000 followers seemed attractive. But the influencer's audience interested in fashion and entertainment had virtually no interest in the brand's B2B office supplies.

The collaboration generated impressive reach numbers that looked good in reports. But sales from the partnership were zero. Follower growth during the campaign was substantial at 1,200 new followers, but 90 percent unfollowed within 30 days when they saw the brand's regular content about office productivity and realized the mismatch. The partnership cost time and product samples while delivering nothing of lasting value.

The lesson: quality of audience fit matters more than quantity of reach. Pursue partners whose audiences would genuinely benefit from knowing about you.

| 11 |

Organic Growth Tactics

Inside This Chapter

We examine organic growth tactics that build audiences actually caring about what you offer. The analysis covers sustainable growth expectations at different account stages, common plateau patterns that every account experiences, and the critical difference between follower accumulation and qualified audience development.

Growth at any cost leads to audiences that never convert. Ten thousand followers who ignore your content have less value than one thousand followers who engage, share, and eventually become customers, donors, or community members. Sustainable growth means building audiences that matter for your actual business objectives rather than impressive numbers that deliver nothing.

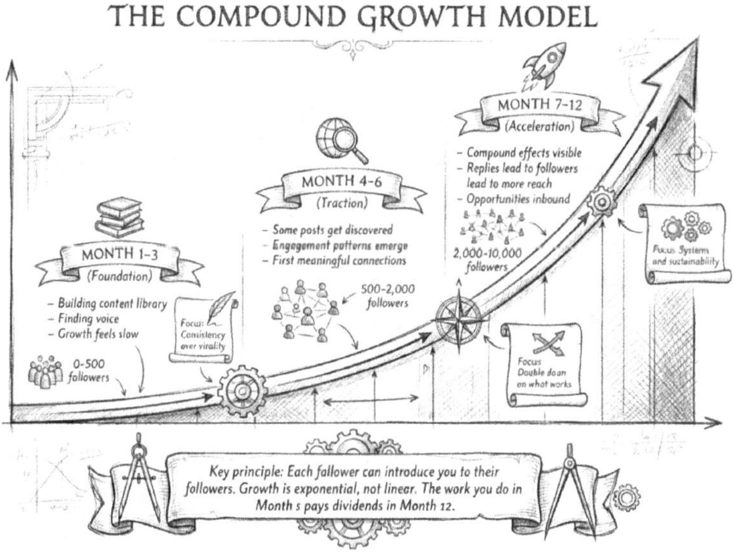

Figure 11.1: The Compound Growth Model

Realistic Growth Expectations

New accounts under 1,000 followers should target 5 to 20 new followers weekly with consistent posting. Growth at this stage is slow because you have limited distribution. The algorithm doesn't know whether to trust your content yet. Your follower base is too small to generate significant engagement that triggers broader distribution. Do not expect viral breakthroughs during this foundation stage.

Focus on establishing posting consistency and refining your content approach during this period. Experiment with different content types, formats, and topics to discover what resonates with your emerging audience. This experimentation matters more than growth metrics at this stage because you're learning what works before scaling.

Accounts between 1,000 and 10,000 followers should target 50 to 200 new followers weekly. Growth accelerates during this stage as content finds its audience and the algorithm begins distributing to larger networks. You have built enough engagement history that the platform trusts your content more. This stage often feels like breaking through a ceiling after months of slower growth.

Accounts above 10,000 followers have potential for rapid growth through viral moments but also face diminishing returns on basic tactics. Simple optimizations that drove earlier growth now provide smaller marginal improvements. Growth becomes about optimization and compounding rather than following formulas. Strategy must evolve to maintain momentum.

Growth rates vary enormously by niche in ways that make universal benchmarks misleading. B2B accounts targeting narrow professional audiences grow slower than consumer lifestyle accounts targeting broad interests. A consultant specializing in non-profit financial management will grow slower than a fitness influencer targeting general health interest. The comparison should be against your own trajectory and relevant competitors in your niche, not generic benchmarks from unrelated industries.

Consistency matters more than speed. Steady growth of 50 followers weekly compounds to 2,600 yearly. Bursts of viral growth followed by dormancy often net less total growth because inactive periods lose followers and damage algorithmic standing. The account that posts consistently for years outperforms the account that goes viral once and then disappears.

The Compound Growth Model

Understanding how growth compounds helps you make patient strategic decisions rather than chasing quick wins that don't last.

Early growth feels slow because you're building from small base. Gaining 20 followers when you have 200 represents 10 percent growth, but the absolute number seems insignificant. This phase requires patience and trust in the process.

Middle growth accelerates as your base grows and content finds audience. The same effort that produced 20 new followers now produces 50 because your content reaches more people and your engagement compounds.

Late growth plateaus as you saturate accessible audience. Eventually you reach most people interested in your specific niche. Further growth requires strategy evolution: expanding topics, paid amplification, or accepting that your niche has natural ceiling.

The patience required: Most accounts give up during early slow growth phase, never reaching acceleration. Those who persist through the slow early months disproportionately benefit from compound growth later. The strategic insight is simple: consistency through slow growth enables eventual acceleration.

Niche Expansion Strategy

When growth plateaus due to niche saturation, strategic expansion into adjacent topics can restart growth without abandoning your positioning.

Adjacent expansion maintains connection to core positioning while reaching new audiences. A pricing strategy consultant might expand into negotiation tactics, still serving professional services but reaching broader audience interested in negotiation. A coffee shop might expand into general food content, still local and food-focused but reaching people interested in food beyond coffee specifically.

Disconnected expansion risks diluting positioning. If the pricing consultant starts posting about fitness or the coffee shop starts posting about politics, they confuse their audience about what to expect. Followers who signed up for specific expertise may unfollow when content drifts too far.

Testing expansion: Before committing to new topics, test with limited content. Post several pieces in the potential expansion area. Monitor engagement and follower response. If expansion content performs well without alienating existing audience, continue. If engagement drops or unfollows increase, pull back.

Common Plateau Patterns

Almost every account experiences growth plateaus. Understanding common patterns helps diagnose and address them rather than abandoning strategy that would work with adjustment.

Content exhaustion plateaus happen when you have covered your core topics thoroughly and fresh angles become difficult to generate. Audiences have heard your main insights expressed various ways. The solution is expanding into adjacent topics that your expertise enables, bringing new perspectives through collaboration or research, or going deeper rather than broader on existing themes to offer advanced insights beyond beginner content.

Audience saturation plateaus happen when you have reached most people interested in your specific niche as you have defined it. Further growth requires either expanding topic scope to interest adjacent audiences, finding new distribution channels beyond organic X reach, or accepting that your niche has a ceiling and optimizing for engagement rather than growth. This plateau is actually a signal of success in your niche, not failure.

Engagement decline plateaus happen when posting continues but engagement drops, signaling content quality or relevance problems. The algorithm distributes less because your existing audience engages less. Your recent content isn't resonating. The solution is content strategy revision based on analyzing what performed well previously, not posting more of what isn't working hoping volume compensates for quality.

Format fatigue plateaus happen when audiences tire of the same content formats repeated endlessly. If every post is a text thread, audiences stop paying attention even if individual threads are good. Introducing video, images, polls, or different structures can restart engagement by providing novelty within your established topics.

Building Qualified Audiences

Follower count means nothing if followers don't care about your work. Vanity metrics that look impressive in reporting deliver no business value. Qualified audience development prioritizes attracting people who will engage, share, and eventually take desired actions.

Content should attract your target audience specifically rather than anyone who might click follow. A business consultant posting entertainment content and industry memes might gain followers who never need consulting services. The growth looks good in weekly reports but delivers no business value because those followers will never become clients.

Engagement quality indicates audience quality more reliably than follower count. Accounts with 10,000 followers and 0.1 percent engagement have worse audiences than accounts with 2,000 followers and 3 percent engagement. The smaller audience cares more and pays attention. They're more likely to click links, remember you, and take action.

Follower source matters for retention and engagement. Followers from viral entertainment posts often unfollow when they see your regular content because they followed for entertainment and got expertise. Followers from valuable niche content stay and engage because they want more of what attracted them initially.

Track not just follower growth but follower quality indicators. Profile visit to follow ratios indicate whether visitors find your profile compelling. Engagement rates over time show whether your audience maintains interest. Website click-through rates reveal whether followers take desired actions. These metrics tell you whether your audience actually cares, not just whether they clicked follow once.

Putting This Into Practice

A nonprofit executive director had been chasing follower count for two years with tactics designed to maximize growth rather than build relevant audience. She hit 15,000 followers but engagement was abysmal at 0.2 percent and donations attributed to X were minimal despite the impressive follower number. Analysis revealed most followers came from viral posts unrelated to the nonprofit's mission: funny observations, trending topic reactions, and entertainment content that attracted general audiences with no interest in affordable housing.

She shifted strategy to focus on mission-aligned content even if growth slowed. Posts about impact stories showing families helped, beneficiary outcomes showing real results, and organizational mission explaining why the work matters replaced the broader entertaining content. She accepted that this shift would cost followers.

Follower growth slowed to half the previous rate as entertainment-seeking followers stopped following and began unfollowing when content shifted. But engagement quadrupled among remaining followers who actually cared about affordable housing.

More importantly, X-attributed donations increased 340 percent as the audience became people who cared about the cause rather than people who thought the executive director was funny.

A consultant experienced similar trajectory through intentional niching. After years of trying to appeal broadly to all business owners, he niched down aggressively to focus exclusively on pricing strategy for professional services firms. Content about general business topics stopped. Every post related to pricing, value positioning, and revenue optimization for consultants and agencies.

Growth seemed to stall initially as broader followers unfollowed and narrower content appealed to smaller audience. Follower count actually declined for two months as the audience self-selected.

But the remaining audience was precisely his target market. Engagement rates climbed to 4 percent as followers genuinely interested in pricing leaned in. Direct inquiries from potential clients increased because everyone following had the exact problem he solved. Within six months, X had become his primary lead source generating $140,000 in attributed revenue despite having fewer followers than his previous peak. Qualified audience beats large audience for business outcomes.

| 12 |

Content Planning for Consistency

Inside This Chapter

We examine how to maintain consistent X presence without exhausting yourself. The analysis covers sustainable posting cadences matched to realistic capacity, energy management across content types requiring different effort levels, and systems preventing the burnout that causes most accounts to go silent.

Most X accounts go silent not because strategy failed but because the person behind them got exhausted. The demands of consistent daily posting, engagement, and content creation overwhelm other responsibilities. The account that seemed manageable in month one becomes burdensome by month four and abandoned by month eight. Sustainable presence requires systems designed around realistic energy capacity rather than aspirational productivity that sounds good but can't be maintained.

Finding Sustainable Cadence

Posting frequency recommendations often assume unlimited time and energy that nobody actually has. The reality is that X competes with your actual job, family responsibilities, health needs, and everything else in your life. Sustainable cadence means the posting frequency you can maintain indefinitely through busy periods and slow periods, not the frequency you can sustain for two weeks before crashing.

For most business accounts managed by one person alongside other responsibilities, 4 to 7 posts weekly provides sufficient visibility without overwhelming demands. This translates to roughly one post daily with occasional days off or planned breaks. The algorithm rewards consistency at this level without requiring the multiple daily posts that would consume available time.

Posting multiple times daily increases visibility but multiplies energy requirements proportionally. Unless X is your primary job responsibility, daily multi-post schedules are unsustainable for most people. Better to post once daily consistently for years than three times daily for months before burning out and going silent for months of recovery.

Chapter 4 details a monthly batching process that makes sustainable cadence achievable. Batching reduces the daily decision load by front-loading content creation into focused sessions, freeing daily energy for engagement rather than creation.

Quality matters more than quantity for both audience value and personal sustainability. One excellent post outperforms five mediocre posts on engagement metrics. But mediocre posts also cost energy to create. If increasing frequency means decreasing quality because you're rushing, don't increase frequency. The diminishing returns aren't worth the additional effort.

Engagement requires separate energy allocation beyond content creation. Creating content is one activity requiring certain mental resources. Engaging with others through replies and conversations is a different activity drawing from limited daily capacity. Both are necessary for X success but both draw from the same finite pool of time and attention. Account for engagement time when planning sustainable workflow.

Energy Management Across Content Types

Different content types require different energy and time investments. Understanding this variation helps you allocate effort strategically across days and weeks.

Text posts require the lowest production energy of any content type. A text post can be written in five minutes during brief breaks, making text your sustainable baseline: the content type you can produce even on difficult days when energy is low. When you have nothing else, a text post maintains presence.

Images require moderate production energy. Finding or creating appropriate images, ensuring quality and dimensions, and uploading alongside text takes more time than text alone. Save image posts for days with more capacity when you can invest the additional effort.

Video requires the highest production energy of standard content types. Even simple talking head videos require setup, recording, review, often multiple takes, and sometimes editing. Reserve video production for planned sessions when you have protected time rather than daily creation attempts that will fail.

Threads require extended creative energy beyond single posts. Structuring 5 to 10 connected tweets coherently, ensuring each works independently while contributing to the whole, takes more cognitive effort than single posts even if each individual tweet is simple. Batch thread creation during high energy periods like planned content sessions rather than trying to create threads spontaneously.

Build content calendars reflecting energy reality rather than aspiration. Schedule video production for days you can protect time. Schedule text posts for busy days when only low effort content is realistic. Match content type to anticipated energy availability across your week.

Systems Preventing Burnout

Content banks prevent the daily pressure of creation that causes most burnout. Having 20 to 30 drafted posts ready means you can publish even when you can't create new content. Difficult days draw from the existing bank rather than requiring fresh production under pressure. The buffer absorbs variation in your energy and availability.

Batching reduces total energy expenditure compared to distributed creation. Context switching between tasks consumes energy invisibly. Getting into creative mode costs energy. Getting interrupted and returning costs more energy. Creating 10 posts in one focused session takes less total energy than creating 10 posts across 10 separate sessions that each require getting into and out of creative mode.

Protect batching time as non-negotiable rather than scheduling it hopefully and letting other demands override. The two to three hours of monthly batching prevents far more than two to three hours of daily struggle.

Scheduled breaks prevent accumulated exhaustion that eventually forces involuntary breaks. Plan one week quarterly where you post minimal or pre-scheduled content only while taking break from active creation. This deliberate recovery prevents the gradual energy depletion that eventually forces longer involuntary breaks when you completely burn out.

Delegation or automation for repetitive tasks preserves creative energy for content that requires your unique voice. If scheduling, analytics review, or routine engagement can be delegated to team members or systematized through tools, reserve your energy for creative work that only you can do.

Permission to reduce temporarily prevents complete abandonment. When life demands attention elsewhere through family emergencies, health issues, or work crises, reduce posting frequency rather than stopping entirely. Three posts weekly is better than zero posts for three weeks. Consistency at reduced volume maintains algorithmic standing and audience connection better than disappearance followed by attempted comeback.

The Sustainable Creator Framework

Long-term X success requires treating content creation as a sustainable practice rather than a heroic effort. This framework ensures you can maintain presence for years rather than burning out in months.

Define your minimum viable presence: the posting frequency you can maintain during your worst weeks when everything else demands attention. For most people, this is 2 to 3 posts weekly. This minimum becomes your floor, the level you never drop below even in crisis.

Define your optimal presence: the posting frequency that generates strong results during normal weeks when you have adequate time and energy. For most people, this is 5 to 7 posts weekly. This optimal becomes your target for planning purposes.

Define your peak capacity: the posting frequency you can sustain during your best weeks when inspiration flows and time is available. For most people, this is daily or even multiple posts daily. This peak should feel energizing rather than exhausting.

Operate mostly at optimal, occasionally at peak, and never below minimum. When you notice yourself dipping toward minimum, that's a signal to protect energy rather than push harder. Pushing through exhaustion leads to the complete stops that damage accounts more than reduced posting would.

Recovery Protocols

When burnout warning signs appear, implement recovery protocols before you completely stop:

Warning signs include dreading X rather than enjoying it, publishing content you aren't proud of just to maintain schedule, engagement feeling like obligation rather than conversation, creative ideas not flowing during batching sessions, and physical symptoms of stress when thinking about posting.

First-level response: Reduce to minimum viable presence for two weeks. Post only content already created. Limit engagement to responses rather than proactive conversation. Use the freed time for activities that restore energy.

Second-level response: Take one week completely off from X. Schedule minimum content if possible, or simply accept a week of silence. Remove X from your phone temporarily. Return only when you feel genuinely ready rather than obligated.

Third-level response: Reassess whether X serves your goals at all. If repeated burnout occurs despite systems, perhaps the platform isn't right for your working style, or perhaps your goals don't require X presence. Permission to quit entirely is always available.

Putting This Into Practice

A solo consultant maintained consistent presence through a major personal crisis using layered systems built before the crisis occurred. When a family emergency demanded full attention for three weeks, she had content banked from previous batching sessions. Scheduled posts continued publishing automatically. Engagement was minimal as she had no time to reply or interact, but basic presence continued.

When the crisis resolved, she resumed normal workflow without rebuilding lost momentum. The audience barely noticed disruption because content had continued. The algorithmic standing remained intact because posting had not stopped. The systems absorbed disruption that would have silenced accounts without such preparation.

A nonprofit communications director found burnout through over-ambition despite good intentions. Committed to posting three times daily to maximize reach, she maintained the pace for four months through significant personal effort. By month five, she was exhausted. X began feeling like burden rather than opportunity.

The account went silent for two months while she recovered. Returning felt overwhelming because the silence had damaged momentum and she felt pressure to compensate. The account lost significant following during absence as followers unfollowed inactive accounts. Rebuilding engagement capacity took additional months.

She rebuilt with sustainable expectations: one post daily maximum, engagement limited to 20 minutes daily, batching limited to 90 minutes weekly. Two years later, the account had surpassed her previous peak follower count and engagement rates with a fraction of previous effort. The sustainable pace enabled consistency that ambitious scheduling had destroyed.

| 13 |

Metrics & Analytics That Drive Decisions

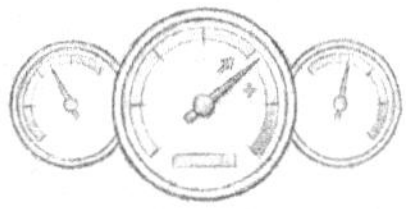

Inside This Chapter

We examine which metrics actually matter and how to build analytics systems that enable decisions rather than just creating impressive reports. The analysis covers distinguishing vanity metrics from value metrics, building dashboard systems for different decision timeframes, and attribution tracking that connects X activity to business outcomes.

You invest hours weekly creating content and engaging with community. Your follower count grows. Your engagement increases. But when asked whether X contributes meaningfully to business results, you have no compelling answer beyond "I think it helps." Analytics transform vague impressions into concrete evidence that justifies continued investment.

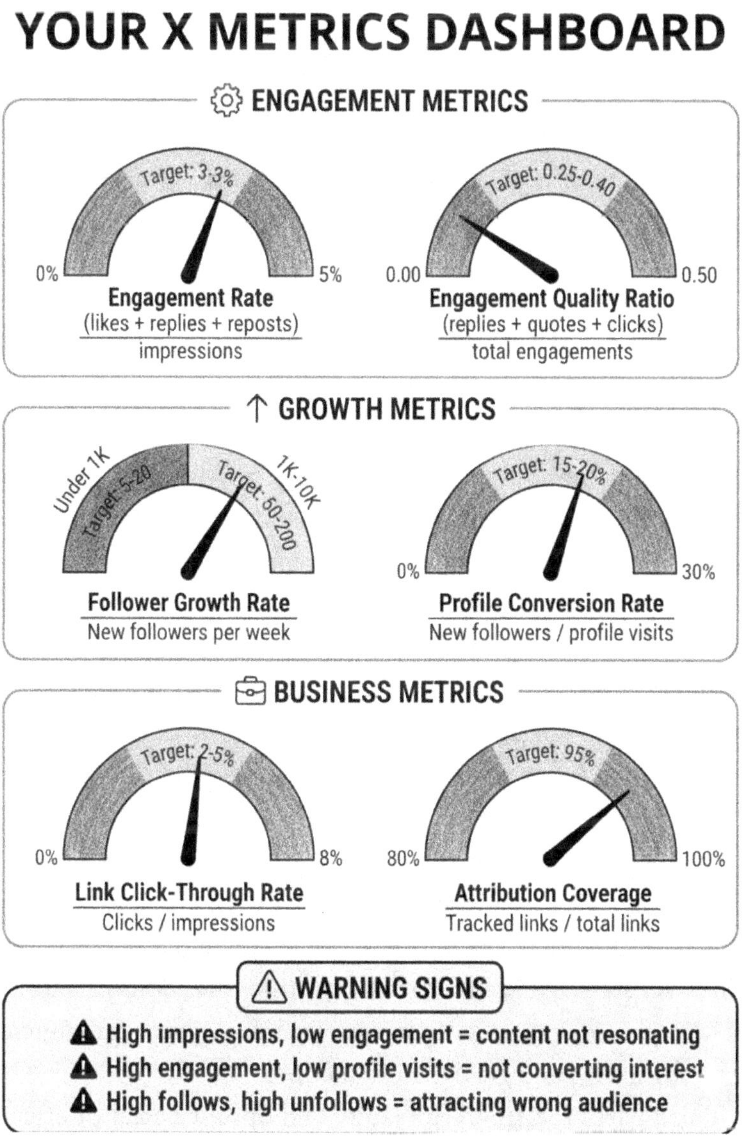

Figure 13.1: Your X Metrics Dashboard

What You Can Measure

X provides tiered analytics access based on account type that determines what data you can access.

Free accounts receive basic post level metrics visible on individual posts: impressions showing how many times the post was seen, engagements showing total interactions, engagement rate showing the ratio of engagements to impressions, link clicks, and profile visits. These metrics enable rudimentary performance assessment but lack historical tracking, demographic insights, or comparative analysis across time periods. Free analytics suffice for casual personal accounts but limit strategic optimization for business use.

Premium subscribers at $8 monthly gain access to comprehensive X Analytics dashboard with significantly more capability. Historical data shows performance trends over time rather than just recent posts. Audience demographics reveal follower locations, interests, gender distribution, and household income brackets where available. The dashboard organizes data into useful sections: Home tab providing 28-day overview, Tweets tab showing individual post performance with sorting capability, Audiences tab revealing follower characteristics, and Video Activity tab isolating video specific metrics.

Premium Plus at $40 monthly adds enhanced benchmarking and deeper audience insights. However, the incremental analytics value over standard Premium rarely justifies the additional cost for analytics purposes alone. Standard Premium provides sufficient depth for most strategic decision making.

Third party tools like Hootsuite and Sprout Social offer cross platform reporting covering all your social accounts, competitive benchmarking against similar accounts, and customizable dashboards organizing data as you prefer. These cost $30 to $500 plus monthly depending on features and team size. Most accounts should master native Analytics before investing in third party tools to ensure the investment solves actual problems rather than creating impressive unused dashboards.

Vanity Versus Value Metrics

Vanity metrics are easily visible, psychologically satisfying, and fun to watch grow. They look good in reports and feel like progress. But they weakly correlate with business outcomes. Follower count, raw like counts, and total impressions can all grow while business results remain flat.

A viral post generating one million impressions and 10,000 likes delivers no business value if it attracts unqualified audience with no interest in what you offer. Accounts optimizing for vanity metrics often experience impressive follower growth without corresponding increases in website traffic, leads, or revenue. The metrics look good while business impact remains minimal.

Value metrics connect directly to business objectives and show actual progress toward goals that matter. Conversion rate measures desired actions completed relative to opportunities. Cost per acquisition tracks efficiency of customer generation. Engagement quality ratio separates meaningful interactions showing genuine interest from passive likes that require no thought. Revenue attribution connects actual sales to X activity.

Calculate your engagement quality ratio by adding replies plus quote posts plus link clicks, then dividing by total engagements. This ratio separates high investment interactions from low investment likes. Ratios above 0.30 indicate high quality engagement where audiences actively respond and take action. Ratios below 0.15 suggest engagement consists primarily of passive likes from disengaged scrollers. Ten meaningful replies that become conversations matter more than 100 passive likes from people who will never remember your content.

Track engagement quality ratio monthly. Target 0.25 to 0.40 indicating balanced mix of appreciation and active engagement. If ratio falls below 0.20, diagnose which component drives the problem: weak calls to action reducing link clicks, insufficient conversation prompts reducing replies, or lack of shareworthy insights reducing quote posts. Optimize the specific weakness rather than pursuing generic engagement increases.

Building Your Dashboard

Avoid data overwhelm through tiered review systems that match different decision timeframes and depths.

Daily operational review takes 5 minutes maximum. Check yesterday's post performance to spot any unusual results. Respond to comments requiring response. Note anomalies worth investigating later. Don't analyze patterns or draw conclusions. Just maintain awareness of recent activity.

Weekly tactical review takes 30 minutes. Analyze the past 7 days compared to previous weeks to spot emerging trends. Identify top performing content from the week and consider why it worked. Note engagement patterns across days and times. Make small adjustments for the coming week based on observations.

Monthly strategic review takes 90 minutes and drives larger decisions. Conduct deep analysis of the past 30 days examining patterns invisible in weekly data. Review audience growth and quality trends over the full period. Assess whether current strategy serves business objectives. Make larger strategic decisions about content pillars, posting cadence, or platform investment based on month-over-month comparisons.

This tiered approach prevents both analysis paralysis from too much data and flying blind from too little attention. Different decisions require different data depth at different frequencies. Daily decisions should not require monthly analysis. Monthly strategy shouldn't rely on yesterday's performance alone.

Setting Up Proper Tracking

Effective analytics requires setup before you need the data. These implementation steps ensure you have useful information when optimization questions arise.

X Analytics access: Verify you have Premium subscription if you want full analytics access. Free accounts receive limited data. Go to Analytics from your profile menu and ensure data is populating correctly. Historical data only begins accumulating once you access the dashboard, so activate it early.

UTM parameter standards: Establish consistent naming conventions before you need them. Standard format: utm_source=twitter (or x), utm_medium=social, utm_campaign=[descriptive campaign name], utm_content=[post description or ID]. Document conventions so all team members use identical parameters. Inconsistent naming creates data fragmentation preventing useful analysis.

Google Analytics configuration: Create custom segments filtering for Twitter/X traffic specifically. Set up goals tracking conversions you care about: email signups, contact form submissions, purchases. Configure attribution windows appropriate for your sales cycle.

Tracking spreadsheet: Create a simple spreadsheet documenting every campaign, link, and UTM parameter used. Include columns for date, campaign purpose, full URL with parameters, and notes about results. This documentation prevents "mystery traffic" from untracked links.

Building Your Analytics Dashboard

Effective dashboards organize data for decisions rather than comprehensive data dumps that overwhelm.

Daily dashboard requires only key operational metrics visible at a glance: yesterday's post performance (impressions and engagement rate), response queue (mentions requiring reply), and any anomalies flagged by your monitoring.

Weekly dashboard adds tactical depth: 7-day engagement trend compared to previous week, top and bottom performing posts from the week, follower growth rate compared to baseline, and content pillar performance breakdown.

Monthly dashboard provides strategic overview: 30-day trends across all key metrics, month-over-month comparisons, content type analysis (which formats perform best), audience demographic changes, and conversion funnel metrics from impression through business outcome.

Build dashboards progressively starting with daily view. Add weekly analysis once daily review is habitual. Add monthly strategic review once weekly analysis is consistent. Attempting comprehensive dashboards before establishing basic habits leads to abandonment.

Attribution Troubleshooting

Common attribution problems and their solutions:

Problem: Traffic from X shows as direct or unknown in Google Analytics. Solution: Verify UTM parameters are properly formatted and included on all links. Check that parameters aren't being stripped by link shorteners.

Problem: Conversions happen but can't be connected to X. Solution: Implement post-purchase surveys asking discovery source. Train sales team to ask how prospects found you. Create X-exclusive offers with unique codes proving origin.

Problem: X-attributed revenue seems too low relative to effort. Solution: Consider attribution window. Multi-touch journeys may credit other channels for conversions X initiated. Implement longer attribution windows or multi-touch models if your sales cycle exceeds typical attribution periods.

Problem: Data exists but doesn't drive decisions. Solution: Calculate your data-to-action ratio. Track how often analytics review leads to specific strategy changes. If ratio is low, simplify dashboards to focus only on actionable metrics. Remove metrics that inform but never influence decisions.

Attribution Tracking

X rarely drives immediate conversion for most businesses. The typical customer journey involves multiple touchpoints: discovering your brand through a post, visiting your profile to learn more, clicking to your website, leaving without converting, returning days later via search or email, then finally purchasing. The person who bought may not even remember that X started the journey.

Traditional X Analytics can't track this multi-touch attribution, reporting only direct link clicks that happened immediately. Research suggests social media influences roughly 31 percent of B2B purchase decisions but receives direct attribution for only 6 percent of conversions when measured through last click attribution. The gap exists because social media often starts journeys that other channels close.

Implement comprehensive attribution through three complementary mechanisms. First, add UTM parameters to all X links enabling Google Analytics to track traffic source precisely: utm_source=twitter, utm_medium=social, utm_campaign=[campaign_name]. Use consistent naming conventions so data aggregates properly. Second, create unique promotional codes mentioned only on X proving platform specific conversions that couldn't have come from anywhere else. Third, add post-purchase survey questions asking "How did you first hear about us?" to capture assisted conversions that technical tracking misses.

Calculate attribution coverage: link clicks with proper UTM tracking divided by total link clicks. Target 95 percent coverage ensuring nearly all traffic is trackable to source and eventual outcomes.

Putting This Into Practice

A SaaS company couldn't show X value to leadership despite active presence and apparent engagement. When budget reviews asked for justification, no attribution system existed to prove business impact. Leadership questioned continued investment.

They implemented systematic attribution. UTM tracking on all links with consistent naming. X-specific landing pages that only appeared through X traffic. Sales team training to ask discovery source during demos. Monthly attribution reporting showing traced journey from X post to demo to close.

Over six months, they documented $200,000 in pipeline directly attributable to X through rigorous tracking. Further analysis revealed average deal from X traffic was 23 percent larger than deals from other sources, possibly because X content pre-qualified buyers who understood the product before reaching sales. Leadership not only approved continued investment but increased budget based on showed ROI.

A consultant with strong engagement discovered through segmented analysis that case study posts drove 4.2 times more consultation requests than thought leadership posts despite thought leadership posts generating higher engagement metrics including more likes and impressions. The posts that looked better by vanity metrics performed worse on business outcomes.

She shifted content allocation from 15 percent to 35 percent case studies, accepting lower engagement metrics in exchange for higher conversion rates. Consultation requests increased 65 percent the following quarter. The lesson: aggregate metrics hide actionable insights. Segmented analysis by content type reveals which specific content drives business results versus which generates impressive but empty engagement.

| 14 |

Monetizing Your X Efforts

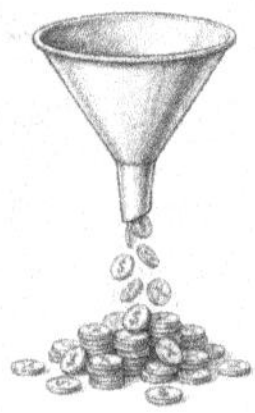

Inside This Chapter

We examine how to generate revenue from X presence without destroying the audience trust that makes revenue possible. The analysis covers Creator Revenue Sharing realities and realistic income expectations, indirect monetization through business development and lead generation, and the economics of sponsored content for accounts with established audiences.

Your competitor monetizes X generating $8,000 monthly. Your X presence generates followers and goodwill but zero dollars. This chapter teaches ethical monetization approaches that build rather than burn audience trust while generating returns on your content investment.

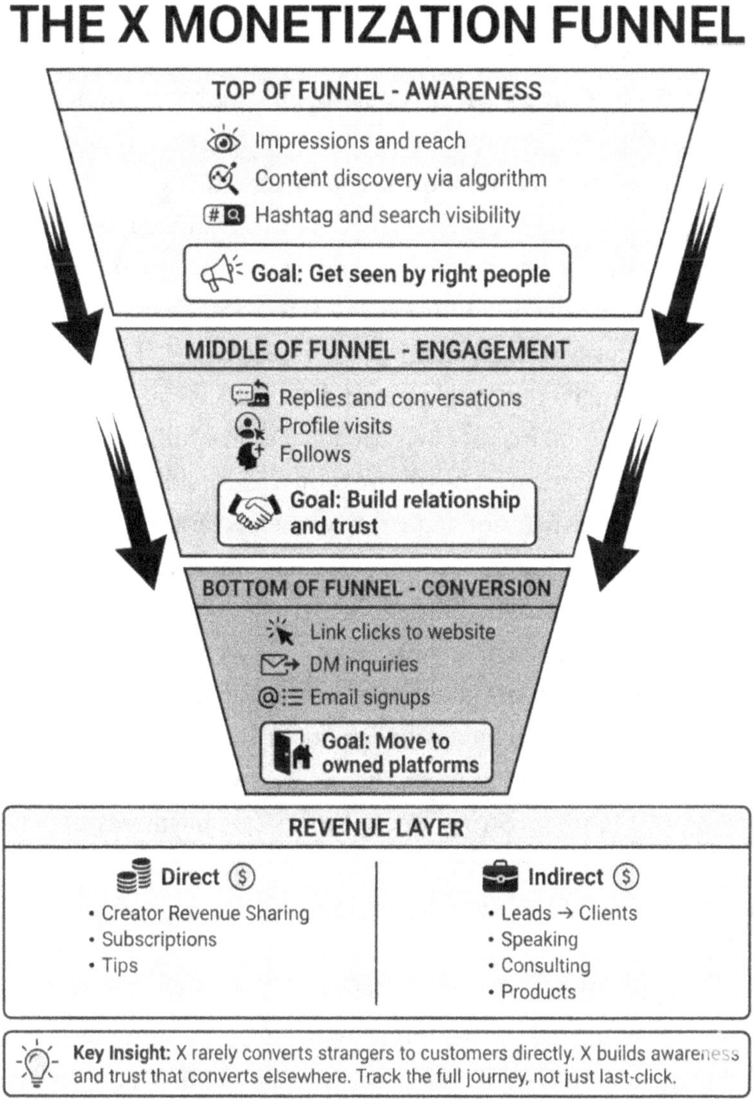

Figure 14.1: The X Monetization Funnel

Creator Revenue Sharing Reality

Premium and Premium Plus subscriptions unlock eligibility for X's Creator Revenue Sharing program, but eligibility doesn't guarantee meaningful income. Understanding the requirements and realistic expectations prevents disappointment.

Eligibility requires 2,000 verified followers, meaning you must have Premium or Premium Plus subscription to get the follower verification that makes followers count toward the threshold, plus 5 million impressions over the past three months. These thresholds have changed multiple times and may change again, so verify current requirements at help.x.com before building strategy around monetization. The impression threshold is substantial. Five million impressions quarterly means averaging roughly 55,000 daily impressions, far beyond what most business accounts with under 10,000 followers generate.

Revenue comes from ads displayed in reply threads under your posts. When your posts generate conversation and replies, ads appear in those reply threads. You earn a portion of ad revenue from those placements. Distribution happens biweekly via Stripe, requiring you to set up Stripe account to receive payments.

At minimum threshold of 5 million quarterly impressions, expect $50 to $300 monthly depending on your content niche and audience demographics. Technology and business audiences command higher ad rates than entertainment or general interest content. Reaching $1,000 monthly requires sustained high engagement with large audiences, typically 20,000 plus engaged followers generating consistent strong performance.

Creator Revenue Sharing makes sense as bonus income for accounts already generating high engagement naturally through valuable content. The revenue is a nice addition to results you're already achieving. It doesn't make sense as primary motivation for

Premium subscription or X strategy. For most business accounts, indirect monetization through leads, clients, and business development generates far more value than platform payments will ever provide.

Indirect Monetization

The real money from X comes through business it drives rather than platform payments. This indirect monetization often exceeds direct monetization by orders of magnitude.

Leads discover you through content and reach out because your expertise is evident. They arrive pre-qualified because following your content has already established your credibility and showed your approach. Clients who followed your expertise before reaching out require less selling because trust already exists. Speaking invitations come from event organizers who saw your threads and want that perspective on their stage. Consulting inquiries come from executives who read your insights and want that thinking applied to their problems.

A consultant generating $95,000 in client revenue attributed to X, tracked through rigorous source attribution, eclipses what Creator Revenue Sharing could provide at any realistic scale. The indirect value dwarfs direct platform payments.

Track indirect monetization rigorously to understand and optimize it. Ask new clients how they found you during intake conversations. Tag CRM records with acquisition source so you can analyze patterns. Calculate X-attributed revenue quarterly so you can show return on time invested. This documentation justifies continued investment and guides strategy refinement toward content that generates business.

The path to indirect monetization has three components. First, build audience that includes your target customers by posting content they find valuable. Second, show expertise through valuable content so they see you can help them. Third, make it easy for interested parties to take next steps through clear calls to action, accessible contact information, and frictionless paths from follower to inquiry.

Lead Generation Funnel Design

Systematic lead generation from X requires deliberate funnel design rather than hoping followers eventually become customers.

Top of funnel: Content attracts and builds audience. Focus on value delivery that establishes expertise. This stage doesn't sell. It builds trust and shows capability. Metrics: follower growth, engagement rates, audience quality indicators.

Middle of funnel: Content moves interested followers toward action. Case studies showing specific results. Behind-the-scenes looks at your process. Client transformation stories. This stage shows what working with you achieves. Metrics: profile visits, link clicks, email signups.

Bottom of funnel: Direct offers to qualified prospects. Consultation offers to engaged followers. Product launches to warm audience. Service promotions to people who have showed interest. This stage converts. Metrics: inquiries, sales, revenue.

Most accounts over-weight bottom of funnel content, constantly selling to audiences not ready to buy. Effective funnels spend 60 to 70 percent of effort on top and middle, building the audience and trust that makes bottom of funnel content convert.

Pricing Your Expertise

When monetizing through services sold to your X audience, pricing strategy affects both revenue and positioning.

Premium positioning: Higher prices signal expertise and attract clients who value quality over cost. Your X content supporting premium positioning should show sophisticated thinking and significant results. Underpricing while claiming expertise creates credibility dissonance.

Productized services: Packaging expertise into defined offerings with clear prices simplifies buying decisions. "Strategic audit for $500" is easier to buy than "consulting at $200 per hour for however many hours this takes." X content can promote specific packages directly.

Value-based pricing: Pricing based on value delivered rather than time spent enables higher revenue. Your X content should establish the value of outcomes you deliver, making value-based pricing conversations easier. Case studies showing ROI support value-based pricing.

Sponsorship Negotiation

When pursuing sponsored content, negotiation affects both revenue and relationship quality.

Know your value: Calculate your cost per thousand followers and compare to industry benchmarks. Understand your engagement rate relative to competitors. Know your audience demographics and their value to advertisers. This preparation prevents underselling.

Negotiate terms beyond rate: Payment timing, creative control, exclusivity period, and usage rights all matter. Payment upfront or upon posting rather than 30-plus days after. Creative approval ensuring content meets your standards. Reasonable exclusivity periods that don't prevent other opportunities. Usage rights limiting how sponsors can repurpose your content.

Build ongoing relationships: One-time sponsorships provide less value than ongoing partnerships. After successful sponsored content, propose ongoing relationship: recurring posts, ambassador arrangement, or retainer relationship. Ongoing relationships provide predictable income and reduce constant sales effort.

Sponsored Content Economics

Accounts with established audiences can monetize through brand partnerships where companies pay you to mention or feature their products to your followers. Rates depend on follower count, engagement rates, and audience demographics.

Micro-influencers with 10,000 to 50,000 followers typically command $100 to $500 per sponsored post. Mid-tier accounts with 50,000 to 200,000 followers command $500 to $2,000. Larger accounts negotiate individually based on specific campaign value and audience quality metrics.

Sponsored content requires disclosure. FTC guidelines and X policies mandate clear labeling of paid partnerships. Non-disclosure damages credibility when discovered, and discovery is increasingly common as audiences become more sophisticated about spotting unmarked sponsorships. Regulatory action is also possible for undisclosed material relationships.

The economics only work sustainably when sponsorships align with audience interests. Promoting products your audience doesn't care about generates revenue once while destroying trust permanently. Followers recognize irrelevant sponsorships and lose faith in your recommendations. Successful creators only accept partnerships genuinely relevant to their community and decline lucrative offers that would alienate their audience.

Putting This Into Practice

A business consultant with 6,500 followers had strong engagement but X generated no direct revenue. The audience was engaged but no money flowed from that engagement.

She implemented systematic lead generation integrated into her content strategy. Weekly office hours threads invited questions from followers, showing expertise publicly while identifying potential clients through their questions. Valuable content ended with soft consultation offers: "If you're dealing with this at your company, I'd be happy to discuss your specific situation." Rigorous source tracking on all inquiries identified which leads came from X.

Over 18 months of consistent execution, meaningful X-attributed revenue becomes achievable. Thirty-eight percent of new clients cited X as discovery source when asked during intake. The monetization came not from platform features or sponsored content but from building audience that included her target market and making it easy for that market to become clients.

A content creator with 25,000 followers explored sponsorship opportunities as primary monetization approach. She developed a rate card based on her engagement metrics to share with potential sponsors. She proactively approached 10 brands whose products aligned with her audience's interests rather than waiting for inbound inquiries. She established disclosure protocols exceeding FTC requirements to protect audience trust.

Three sponsored relationships generated $3,500 monthly from posts featuring tools and services her audience genuinely benefited from knowing about. Creator Revenue Sharing added $260 monthly. Total X monetization reached $3,760 monthly while maintaining audience trust through relevant partnerships and transparent disclosure. The key was selectivity: she declined far more sponsorship offers than she accepted, taking only partnerships where she would genuinely recommend the product regardless of payment.

| 15 |

Challenges and Risks on X

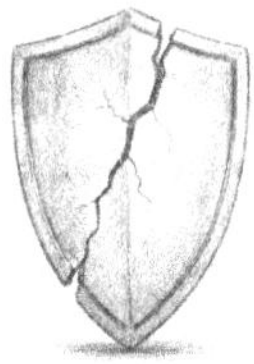

Inside This Chapter

We examine the risks that can destroy years of progress on X. The analysis covers account security protecting against compromise, content policy navigation avoiding suspension, reputation management in public spaces, and crisis response planning before crises occur.

Your account gets suspended. You have no idea why. Three years of audience building vanishes overnight. Appeals go unanswered for weeks. This chapter teaches risk identification and mitigation that protects your X investment from preventable disasters.

Account Security

Account compromise is more common than most users realize. Phishing attacks arrive disguised as legitimate X communications. Weak passwords fall to automated testing. Third party apps granted account access years ago can be compromised or turn malicious. Once compromised, accounts can be used to spam your followers, held for ransom, or simply destroyed by attackers with no interest in negotiation.

Enable two factor authentication immediately if you haven't already. This single step prevents most unauthorized access by requiring both password and a second verification. Use an authenticator app rather than SMS for the second factor. SMS is vulnerable to SIM swapping attacks where criminals convince phone companies to transfer your number, receiving your verification codes.

Review authorized apps quarterly by visiting Settings and Privacy, then Security and account access, then Apps and sessions. Third party tools granted account access during previous experiments or jobs can be compromised or could turn malicious through ownership changes. Remove any apps you no longer actively use or don't recognize from their names.

Document your account recovery information so you can access it during emergencies. Know your recovery email and ensure you still have access to that email account. Know your phone number on file and ensure it is current. Store backup codes securely outside of your phone in case your phone is lost or compromised. If you lose access, this documentation enables faster recovery through X support.

Create recovery plan before you need it. Who has access credentials besides you? Where are backup codes stored? What is the process for reporting compromise to X? Having answers ready before crisis occurs enables faster response than figuring things out whilc panicking.

Content Policy Risks

X enforces content policies that can result in warnings, temporary suspensions, or permanent account termination. Understanding the boundaries prevents accidental violations that put your account at risk.

Automation policies restrict scheduled posting frequency and automated interactions. Excessive automation through dozens of scheduled posts firing simultaneously or automated replies and follows triggers spam detection systems. Keep scheduled posts to reasonable volumes spread across time rather than concentrated bursts. Avoid any automated engagement that mimics human interaction.

Impersonation policies prohibit accounts misleading users about identity. Parody and fan accounts must be clearly labeled as parody or fan accounts to avoid confusion. Business accounts must represent actual businesses rather than impersonating other companies. Using competitor names or similar handles invites policy action.

Manipulation policies target coordinated inauthentic behavior designed to artificially inflate engagement or reach. Purchasing followers violates terms and provides no lasting value anyway because purchased followers don't engage. Engagement pods where groups artificially boost each other's content violate terms. Automated likes and reposts from services violate terms. These shortcuts risk account termination while providing no genuine audience building.

Sensitive content policies restrict certain content types and require appropriate labeling on others. Understand the boundaries for your industry. When in doubt about whether specific content violates policies, err toward caution or contact X support for clarification before posting.

Reputation Risks

Public presence on X creates reputation vulnerability that private communication doesn't carry. Past statements resurface when you become more visible. Context collapses as content reaches audiences beyond those you intended. Screenshots preserve statements forever even after deletion.

Audit your posting history periodically using X's search of your own posts. Look for content that could damage your current reputation or be taken out of context. Remove or address problematic content proactively. What seemed acceptable or funny years ago may not serve your current professional positioning.

Establish response protocols before crises occur so you aren't creating policy under pressure. Know who in your organization has authority to respond to public criticism. Have pre-approved messaging templates for common scenarios like customer complaints, factual errors, or controversial statements. Speed matters in crisis response, and pre-approval enables speed.

Separate personal opinion from professional identity intentionally rather than discovering boundaries through costly mistakes. Some accounts maintain strict professional boundaries, posting only about their area of expertise and avoiding personal or political content entirely. Others embrace personal expression as part of authentic connection. Either approach can work, but decide your approach deliberately and maintain it consistently.

Crisis Response

When crises occur, response speed and approach determine outcome more than the underlying facts of the situation.

Acknowledge issues quickly rather than hoping they disappear. Silence amplifies speculation as people assume the worst about why you aren't responding. Even if you can't provide full resolution immediately, acknowledging awareness shows responsiveness. "We're aware of [issue] and investigating" buys time while showing you aren't hiding.

Take responsibility where appropriate rather than becoming defensive. Defensive responses often escalate situations as critics double down against perceived deflection. Genuine accountability frequently defuses anger because people want acknowledgment more than punishment. "We made a mistake. Here is what happened and what we're doing to fix it" resolves most situations that defensive responses would prolong.

Move extended disputes to private channels once initial public acknowledgment has been made. Public arguments rarely benefit anyone and provide entertainment for observers while damaging all participants. Offer to continue conversation via direct message or email where nuance is possible and spectators aren't inflaming the situation.

Document everything during crises. Screenshot the original issue, your responses, and eventual resolution. This documentation protects you if situations escalate, recur, or require legal attention. Memory is unreliable under stress, so contemporary documentation proves essential.

Security Implementation Checklist

Comprehensive security requires implementing multiple layers rather than relying on single protections.

Account security: Enable two-factor authentication using authenticator app rather than SMS. Use unique strong password not used anywhere else. Enable login verification alerts. Review and revoke unnecessary authorized apps quarterly.

Recovery preparation: Document recovery email and ensure access. Document phone number on file and ensure current. Store backup codes securely outside your phone. Know recovery process before you need it.

Monitoring: Set up Google Alerts for your name and brand. Use social listening tools to detect unusual account activity. Monitor follower count for unexpected drops that might indicate issues.

Team access: If multiple people access the account, use X's Teams features rather than sharing passwords. Implement access controls limiting who can publish. Review access permissions when team members change roles.

Content Policy Navigation

Avoiding policy violations requires understanding boundaries in your specific content area.

Automated content: X restricts automated posting that mimics human behavior. Scheduled posts are fine. Automated replies, automated follows, and artificial engagement violate policy. Even well-intentioned automation can trigger enforcement.

Political content: X has specific rules for political advertising and content from political accounts. If your content touches political topics, understand the boundaries. Disclosure requirements may apply.

Regulated industries: Financial services, healthcare, and other regulated industries have additional content restrictions both from X and from industry regulators. Ensure compliance with all applicable requirements.

When uncertain: X provides policy documentation at help.x.com. If specific content types raise questions, review policy documentation or consider consulting with platform specialists before publishing content that could trigger enforcement.

Crisis Communication Templates

Having pre-approved response templates enables fast, professional crisis response.

Customer complaint template: "Thank you for bringing this to our attention. We take [issue] seriously. I'd like to look into your specific situation, could you DM us your [identifying information]? We'll follow up within [timeframe]."

Factual error template: "You're right, and I appreciate the correction. [The correct information is X]. I've updated the original post and apologize for any confusion."

Controversial statement response: "I understand this perspective sparked strong reactions. To clarify my intent: [explanation]. I appreciate the dialogue and am open to continuing the conversation."

No-comment situations: "Thank you for your interest in this topic. I'm not able to comment on [subject] at this time, but I appreciate you reaching out."

Customize templates for your voice and common scenarios. Having templates doesn't mean responses should feel canned; templates provide starting points for faster, more consistent crisis response.

Putting This Into Practice

A tech startup lost account access for 72 hours through a phishing attack disguised as X support communication. The attacker used the compromised account to post spam, damaging brand reputation as followers received unwanted promotional content. Recovery required proving identity to X support, a process complicated by incomplete recovery documentation and confusion about which email was associated with the account.

Post-recovery, they implemented comprehensive security measures to prevent recurrence. They made two-factor authentication via authenticator app mandatory on all team accounts. Documented recovery processes including current phone numbers and backup codes stored in company password manager. Brand monitoring alerts through third party service to detect unusual posting activity. Quarterly authorized app reviews removing unused integrations. Eighteen months later, no subsequent incidents had occurred.

A financial services firm developed crisis protocols before needing them, building playbooks for various scenarios during a calm strategy session. When unexpected market volatility triggered customer anxiety and angry posts questioning the firm's advice, their team responded within 28 minutes using pre-approved messaging that acknowledged concern while providing factual context. Zero compliance violations occurred despite rapid response because messaging had been pre-cleared by compliance during playbook development. Customer sentiment remained positive throughout because quick, professional response showed the firm was paying attention and cared.

The lesson in both cases: prepare before crises arrive. Protocols developed under pressure when emotions run high are worse than protocols developed deliberately when you can think clearly. The time to build your fire escape is before the building is on fire.

| 16 |

X Ads & Promoted Posts

Inside This Chapter

We examine paid advertising on X and when it makes sense for your business. The analysis covers campaign objectives and their different costs, targeting architecture determining who sees your ads, creative requirements for effective ads, and budget optimization to generate measurable returns rather than burning money without outcomes.

You built organic presence methodically over months. Posts reach followers reliably. Conversations generate engagement. Thought leadership earns recognition. Then growth plateaus. Follower acquisition slows despite consistent posting. Website traffic remains insufficient for business goals. Organic reach hits its natural ceiling governed by algorithmic limits and follower behavior beyond your control.

This plateau signals a transition point, not failure. Organic strategy built foundation establishing credibility, content quality, and audience understanding. Paid advertising accelerates growth by reaching audiences beyond your follower base who would never discover you organically, testing messages at scale to find what resonates, and generating measurable conversions from expanded reach.

Understanding Campaign Economics

Campaign economics start with objective selection. X structures campaigns around three categories with distinct optimization behaviors and cost structures.

Awareness objectives maximize impressions and reach, optimizing for getting your ad seen by as many people as possible. These campaigns build brand recognition and audience familiarity supporting later conversion efforts. Average costs run $0.75 to $2.50 per 1,000 impressions depending on targeting precision and creative quality. Awareness campaigns work well for new product launches, brand building initiatives, or building audiences you can retarget later with conversion campaigns. Evaluate awareness campaigns on downstream effects rather than immediate actions because awareness creates foundation for later conversion.

Consideration objectives drive specific engagement actions including post engagement, video views, website traffic, app installs, or follower growth. Platform algorithms optimize toward your selected action, making objective alignment with goals critical. Average costs vary significantly by action type: $0.13 to $0.30 per engagement, $0.02 to $0.10 per video view measured at two seconds or more, $0.40 to $1.20 per website click, $2.50 to $7.00 per new follower. Consideration campaigns generate qualified audiences showing interest through deliberate actions, creating warmer prospects for conversion campaigns.

Conversion objectives generate purchases, signups, form submissions, or other completion actions tracked through X pixel implementation on your website. Platform algorithms optimize delivery toward users most likely to complete conversion actions based on behavioral patterns. Average costs range $2.00 to $6.00 per conversion depending on offer complexity and audience targeting. Conversion campaigns deliver highest business value but require sufficient budget for algorithm learning and perform better with warm audiences from consideration campaigns.

Most small business budgets cluster between $100 and $500 monthly for X advertising. Meaningful results typically require minimum $300 to $500 monthly investment enabling sufficient data collection for algorithm optimization. Campaigns under $10 daily struggle to exit learning phase where algorithms gather performance data, limiting optimization potential and inflating costs.

Campaign Setup Step-by-Step

Proper campaign structure determines success more than creative or targeting alone. Follow this setup process for new campaigns.

Access X Ads Manager through your X account settings or ads.x.com. Create a new campaign and select your objective carefully. Objective selection determines how X's algorithm optimizes delivery.

Campaign level settings: Name your campaign descriptively including objective, target audience, and date for future reference. Set overall campaign budget as daily budget rather than lifetime budget for better control. Set schedule with start date, and end date if applicable.

Ad group level settings: This is where targeting happens. Create targeting based on your strategy: demographics, interests, behaviors, keywords, or custom audiences. Set ad group budget if splitting campaign budget across multiple targeting strategies. Define bidding strategy: automatic bidding works for most campaigns, manual bidding for experienced advertisers wanting more control.

Ad level settings: Upload creative assets. Write ad copy within character limits. Add call to action button appropriate to objective. Preview on multiple device formats before launching.

Launch and monitor: Start with smaller budget to test performance before scaling. Check results after 24 to 48 hours to ensure delivery is occurring. Monitor through learning phase before making optimization decisions.

Targeting Strategy by Business Type

Different businesses require different targeting approaches based on their customer characteristics.

Local businesses: Geographic targeting is primary lever. Use radius targeting around your location. Layer interest targeting relevant to your offering. Exclude areas you don't serve to prevent wasted spend.

B2B services: Target by job titles, industries, and professional interests. Layer behavioral targeting for business decision-makers. Consider keyword targeting around problems you solve. Retarget website visitors from professional contexts.

E-commerce: Interest targeting based on product category. Behavioral targeting for purchase intent signals. Retarget cart abandoners and past customers. Lookalike audiences based on customer lists.

SaaS products: Target by interests aligned with use case. Keyword targeting around problem and solution terms. Retarget free trial users for conversion campaigns. Target competitor audiences through interest and keyword strategies.

Personal brands and creators: Interest targeting aligned with your content niche. Engagement audiences from organic content for retargeting. Lookalike audiences based on your existing followers.

Budget Optimization Strategies

Maximize results from limited budgets through systematic optimization.

Start small and validate before scaling. Initial $15 to $20 daily budget tests whether your targeting and creative work. Scaling budgets that aren't working wastes money. Only increase budgets on campaigns showing positive performance.

Test creative systematically. Run 3 to 5 creative variants against identical targeting. Let each variant accumulate minimum 50 results before comparing. Pause underperformers and reallocate budget to winners. Introduce new creative before fatigue degrades winner performance.

Dayparting optimization: After accumulating performance data, analyze results by time of day and day of week. If certain hours dramatically underperform, exclude them from delivery using scheduling settings. Concentrate budget during high-performance periods.

Audience expansion: Once core targeting proves successful, test expanded audiences. Broaden interests, increase geographic radius, or test lookalike audiences. Monitor performance as audiences expand; some expansion maintains efficiency while other expansion dilutes results.

Funnel budget allocation: Divide budget strategically across funnel stages. Typical allocation: 30 percent awareness building retargeting pools, 40 percent consideration driving engagement and website traffic, 30 percent conversion requesting action from warmed audiences. Adjust based on your specific funnel performance.

Targeting Architecture

Targeting determines campaign efficiency by controlling who sees your ads. Sophisticated targeting reaches qualified audiences likely to care about your offer. Poor targeting burns budget showing ads to broad audiences containing small qualified segments.

Demographic targeting provides foundational segmentation by age ranges, gender, location down to postal code level, language, and device types, establishing boundaries preventing obvious waste like showing local business ads to other countries. But demographic targeting alone provides insufficient precision for most campaigns.

Interest targeting categorizes users into 350 plus categories based on accounts they follow, content they engage with, and topics they search. This reaches audiences showing affinity for relevant topics without requiring them to follow you. Interest targeting typically provides best balance of reach and relevance for most advertisers running their first campaigns.

Behavioral targeting reaches users based on recent actions including event attendance, purchase patterns, or travel activity. Recency matters enormously: users showing relevant behaviors within past seven days convert at three to five times higher rates than users whose relevant behavior was 30 or more days ago. Fresh interest outperforms historical interest.

Keyword targeting displays ads to users recently posting, searching, or engaging with specific keywords. This intent-based targeting reaches people explicitly discussing topics related to your offer, generating highly qualified traffic.

Retargeting reaches users who previously visited your website through X pixel tracking, engaged with your organic content, or appear on customer lists you upload. Retargeting converts at two to three times higher rates than cold prospecting while costing 40 to 60 percent less per acquisition. Warm audiences familiar with your brand convert more easily than cold audiences encountering you for the first time.

Creative and Budget Optimization

Video creative represents the highest impact performancevariable in X advertising. Six to 15 second videos outperform longer alternatives on completion rate and engagement. Include captions because most viewing happens without sound in public or office settings. Feature prominent branding within the first three seconds so viewers know who is speaking even if they don't watch the full video.

Quality scoring affects your costs significantly. X advertising operates on quality-adjusted auction where campaign performance affects cost efficiency. High quality campaigns achieving strong engagement rates pay 30 to 50 percent less per result than low quality campaigns bidding identical amounts. Quality creates compounding advantage where effective creative reduces costs, freeing budget for broader reach.

Start small and scale based on data rather than guessing with large budgets. Launch with $15 to $20 daily budget testing three creative variants against a single audience segment. Run for seven days collecting minimum 50 results enabling meaningful comparison. Analyze which creative performs best, then scale budget gradually on proven winners. Increase 20 percent every three days while monitoring that quality metrics remain stable as you reach broader audience.

Creative fatigue degrades performance 20 to 40 percent after users see the same ad three to five times. Proactive creative refresh every 14 to 21 days maintains momentum by showing audiences fresh content before fatigue sets in.

Sequential funnel architecture achieves two to three times better return than jumping straight to conversion asks with cold traffic. Run awareness campaigns building audiences of people who engaged. Retarget engaged audiences with consideration campaigns driving website visits. Retarget website visitors with conversion campaigns requesting action. This sequential warming produces better results than asking strangers to buy immediately.

Putting This Into Practice

A software company spent $4,000 monthly on X ads with disappointing results: $48 cost per lead against a $40 target that would make the economics work. Analysis revealed the fundamental problem: they were requesting conversions from completely cold audiences who had never heard of them. Ads asked strangers to sign up for demos of a product they did not know existed.

They restructured into sequential campaigns. Awareness campaigns built audiences of people who engaged with educational content about the problem category. Re-targeting campaigns showed product information to people who had engaged with awareness content. Conversion campaigns requesting demo sign-ups only reached people who had visited the website after seeing earlier campaigns.

Cost per lead dropped from $48 to $22, well under the $40 target. The same monthly budget generated nearly twice the leads. Warm audiences who recognized the brand converted far more readily than cold traffic ever had. The additional campaign complexity required more management time but delivered returns justifying the investment.

A local healthcare provider found success through tight geographic targeting rather than funnel sophistication. Tight radius restriction ensured 92 percent of leads were within their service area rather than wasting budget on people who could never become patients. Appointment booking objective outperformed phone call objective by 3.2 times on cost per acquisition, likely because online booking required less friction than phone calls. The resulting cost per new patient was $55 versus $180 industry average reported in benchmarks.

| 17 |

Using AI & Automation Tools

Inside This Chapter

We examine how AI tools can enhance X strategy without replacing the human judgment that makes content valuable. The analysis covers legitimate AI applications that save time, governance requirements preventing quality degradation, and the boundaries between helpful automation and problematic shortcuts.

AI tools promise to write your posts, generate your images, schedule your content, and automate your engagement. Some of these promises deliver genuine value. Others create risks that outweigh benefits. Understanding the difference prevents costly mistakes and wasted investment in tools that hurt more than help.

Where AI Helps

Content ideation benefits significantly from AI assistance. When facing blank page syndrome where no ideas come, AI can generate post ideas, suggest angles on familiar topics, and help brainstorm content themes across your pillars. The ideas generated require human evaluation and refinement, but AI accelerates getting past the blank page to something you can work with.

Drafting assistance works for initial versions that human editors then refine. AI can produce first drafts faster than starting from scratch, handling routine structure and common phrasing. The drafts need substantial revision to match your voice and meet quality standards, but the starting point saves time compared to blank page creation.

Research and summarization benefit from AI's ability to process information quickly. AI can summarize long articles you want to reference, identify key points from multiple sources you're synthesizing, and surface relevant data points for content you're creating. Human verification remains essential because AI may hallucinate facts or miss crucial context, but the research acceleration is real.

Scheduling optimization can use AI to analyze engagement patterns in your historical data and suggest optimal posting times based on when your specific audience is most active. The suggestions provide starting points for testing, though your specific audience may differ from patterns AI identifies.

Analytics interpretation benefits from AI's pattern recognition capabilities. AI can identify trends across your performance data, flag anomalies worth investigating, and spot correlations that might take humans longer to notice scrolling through numbers manually.

AI Tool Selection

The AI tool market changes rapidly. These evaluation criteria help assess tools regardless of which specific products exist when you read this.

Integration with workflow: Does the tool connect to platforms and tools you already use? Standalone tools requiring separate logins and manual content transfer add friction that reduces adoption.

Output quality: Test actual output quality for your use case. Request trial access before purchasing. Evaluate whether outputs require minimal editing or substantial revision.

Customization capability: Can you train the tool on your voice and preferences? Tools that learn from your feedback improve over time. Tools producing generic outputs regardless of input have limited long-term value.

Cost relative to time saved: Calculate time saved per month and multiply by your effective hourly rate. Compare to subscription cost. If tool saves 5 hours monthly and your time is worth $100 per hour, tools costing less than $500 monthly have positive ROI by this calculation.

Privacy and data handling: Where does your content go? Who can access it? Are your inputs used to train models others access? Understand data handling before entrusting strategic content to any platform.

Prompt Engineering for Content

Effective AI prompting significantly improves output quality over generic instructions.

Provide context: Explain who you are, who your audience is, and what purpose the content serves. "I'm a B2B marketing consultant writing for small business owners. I need content that shows expertise while remaining accessible."

Specify format: Describe the exact format you want rather than leaving format decisions to the AI. "Write a thread of 7 posts, each under 250 characters, with a hook first tweet, 5 substantive middle tweets, and a call-to-action final tweet."

Include examples: Show examples of your previous content or content you admire. "Here are three of my best-performing posts for reference. Match this voice and style."

Request options: Ask for multiple versions to choose from rather than single outputs. "Give me three different hook options for this topic so I can choose the strongest."

Iterate and refine: Treat AI outputs as first drafts requiring refinement. Request specific changes. Provide feedback on what worked and what did not. Build iterative prompting into your workflow.

Human-AI Workflow Design

Effective workflows distribute tasks between human and AI based on their respective strengths.

AI strengths: Processing large amounts of information quickly. Generating multiple options for human selection. Handling routine or repetitive phrasing. Summarizing and reformatting content. Identifying patterns in data.

Human strengths: Strategic judgment about what to create. Voice and authenticity that distinguishes your content. Quality assessment of AI outputs. Understanding audience context AI lacks. Making final decisions about publication.

Workflow design: Assign research and initial drafting to AI. Assign voice refinement and strategic decisions to humans. Never publish AI content without human review. Build review into workflow rather than treating it as optional step.

Where AI Creates Risk

Fully automated posting without human review risks quality degradation, voice inconsistency, and potential policy violations. AI doesn't understand your specific brand voice, current context, or audience sensitivities the way you do. AI-generated content requires human oversight before publication to catch errors, tone problems, and contextually inappropriate content.

Automated engagement through AI bots violates X terms of service and damages authenticity. Fake replies that sound generic, automated likes distributed without human decision, and artificial engagement patterns destroy trust when detected. Detection is increasingly sophisticated as platforms invest in identifying inauthentic behavior.

Unverified AI claims create accuracy risks for your credibility. AI confidently generates false information including fabricated statistics, attributed quotes that were never said, and incorrect facts about companies and people. Publishing AI content without fact-checking puts your reputation at risk when followers discover errors.

Voice replacement happens when AI content overwhelms authentic voice in your feed. Audiences follow you for your perspective, experience, and unique way of seeing your industry. AI can't replicate genuine insight drawn from years of experience. If your content increasingly sounds generic because AI generated it, you lose the differentiation that built your audience.

Governance Framework

AI assistance requires governance ensuring human judgment remains sovereign over what gets published. Without governance, the efficiency gains from AI can easily produce quality degradation that costs more than the efficiency saved.

The HAIA-RECCLIN framework assigns clear roles balancing AI capability with human oversight. AI serves defined supporting roles: research assistance finding and organizing information, draft generation creating starting points for human refinement, data analysis processing numbers and identifying patterns. Humans retain decision authority over what gets published, strategic direction for content and positioning, and quality standards that determine what meets your bar.

Every AI-assisted output should pass through human review before publication. This isn't optional overhead that can be skipped when busy. It is essential quality control protecting your reputation and audience trust. Build review into your workflow so AI-generated content automatically queues for human approval rather than publishing directly.

Document AI usage transparently when relevant to your audience. Audiences increasingly expect disclosure of AI assistance in content production. Proactive transparency about how you use AI builds trust rather than creating risk of discovery that damages trust.

Verify all factual claims regardless of source. AI hallucinations are common and often plausible-sounding. Statistics, quotes, company information, and historical facts all require independent verification before publication. Never assume AI-provided facts are accurate.

Putting This Into Practice

A marketing consultant uses AI for initial content drafts that she then substantially revises before posting. The AI generates structure, basic arguments, and common supporting points from her topic prompts. She adds specific insights from her client experience, examples from real situations she has encountered, and voice refinements that match her established tone.

Production time decreased 40 percent while quality remained consistent because human judgment shaped every final output. The efficiency gain came from faster starting points, not reduced quality standards. Every post still receives full human attention before publication.

A nonprofit tried fully automated posting to increase content volume without increasing staff time. They configured AI to generate and publish content based on topic keywords and scheduling parameters. Initial results seemed promising as posting frequency increased.

Engagement dropped 60 percent within six weeks as followers noticed the change. The AI-generated content lacked the authentic voice, specific beneficiary stories, and emotional resonance that had built their audience. Generic AI-produced mission statements replaced compelling human narratives. They returned to human-created content with AI assistance limited to research and ideation phases where AI strength doesn't create voice problems.

The lesson applies broadly: AI tools enhance human capability when governed properly with human decision-making preserved for quality-critical outputs. AI tools degrade results when they replace human judgment for what gets published and how your brand voice sounds.

| 18 |

Putting It All Together

Inside This Chapter

We examine how all elements covered throughout this book work together as integrated strategy rather than disconnected tactics. The analysis synthesizes key principles into actionable framework, provides implementation road-maps for different starting points, and documents real outcomes from systematic application of complete methodology.

You have absorbed seventeen chapters of frameworks, tactics, and principles. Theory proves nothing until tested against reality where competing priorities intrude, resources constrain ambition, and unexpected obstacles force adaptation. This final chapter provides synthesis making implementation practical for your specific situation.

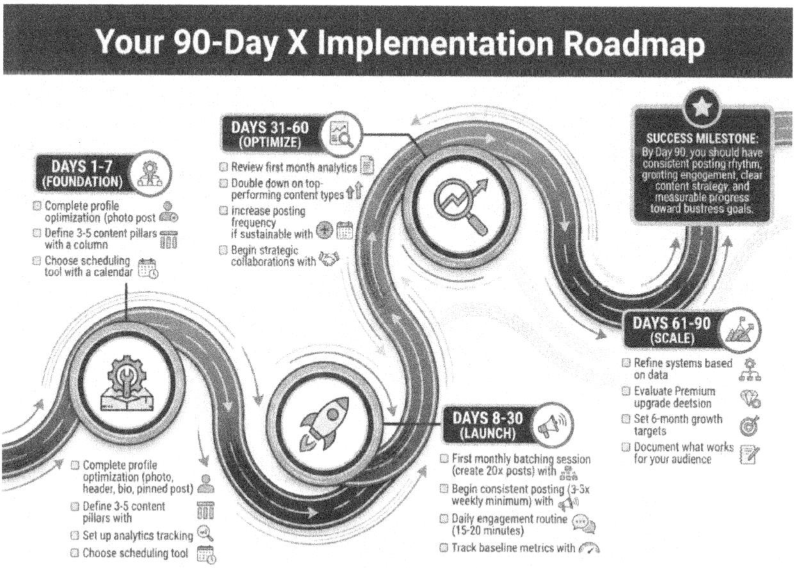

Figure 18.1: Your 90-Day X Implementation Roadmap

The Core Pattern

Successful X presence follows a consistent pattern regardless of context. The specific tactics vary by industry, audience, and resources, but the underlying pattern remains constant.

Profile optimization converts curious visitors to committed followers. Every element of your profile works together to communicate value and inspire follows within seconds of arrival.

Content strategy creates valuable, consistent presence built on pillars that reflect your expertise and audience needs. Planning systems ensure you show up reliably without burning out.

Engagement builds relationships beyond one-way broadcasting. Replies, conversations, and community participation create connection that passive content consumption can't match.

Measurement reveals what works and what wastes time so you can allocate effort intelligently. Analytics guide optimization rather than leaving you guessing about effectiveness.

Iteration improves results over time by applying what measurement reveals. Strategy evolves based on evidence rather than assumptions.

This pattern isn't complicated. The difficulty is execution. Knowing what to do differs from actually doing it consistently over months and years while other responsibilities compete for attention.

Implementation Roadmap

The first 30 days focus on foundation-building rather than results chasing. Complete profile optimization so visitors convert to followers. Establish content pillars organizing your expertise into recognizable themes. Begin posting consistently at sustainable cadence you can maintain indefinitely. Set up analytics tracking before you need the historical data. This phase builds infrastructure that makes later growth possible.

Days 30 to 90 focus on refinement based on emerging data. Analyze what performs and what doesn't. Adjust content mix based on engagement patterns. Increase engagement with others beyond just publishing your own content. Test different formats and posting times to find what works for your specific audience. This phase establishes baseline performance you can optimize against.

Days 90 to 180 focus on optimization accelerating what works. Double down on content types and topics that generate engagement. Eliminate approaches that consume time without results. Explore partnerships expanding reach beyond organic limits. Consider paid amplification for proven content that deserves broader audience. This phase accelerates growth on the foundation earlier phases built.

Beyond 180 days focus on scaling sustainably. Systematize what works through batching, scheduling, and documented processes. Delegate or automate repetitive tasks that don't require your specific expertise. Expand into adjacent opportunities revealed by audience response. This phase builds sustainable presence requiring less effort per result as systems carry more of the load.

90-Day Implementation Plan

This detailed plan transforms book concepts into operational reality over three months.

Days 1 through 7: Foundation. Complete profile optimization using Chapter 2 guidance. Document your content pillars and target percentages. Create initial content bank with 20 ideas per pillar. Set up analytics tracking and document baseline metrics. Make Premium subscription decision based on Chapter 3 framework.

Days 8 through 14: System Setup. Choose and configure scheduling tool based on Chapter 7 guidance. Set up your batching workflow with first monthly session scheduled. Create templates for common content types. Establish tracking spreadsheet for metrics and attribution.

Days 15 through 30: Launch and Learn. Begin posting consistently at your target cadence. Engage with target accounts and communities daily. Track performance daily, compile weekly. Resist optimization urges; gather data first.

Days 31 through 60: Optimize. Analyze first month data to identify patterns. Adjust content mix based on performance. Refine posting times based on engagement patterns. Test different content formats and hooks. Begin partnership identification process.

Days 61 through 90: Accelerate. Double down on content types that work. Eliminate or revise underperformers. Execute initial partnership collaborations. Consider paid amplification for proven content. Assess whether strategy serves business goals.

After 90 days: Review and decide. Calculate ROI across time invested and any financial investment. Determine whether X strategy continues, expands, or stops based on results. If continuing, set goals for next 90 days building on learnings.

Troubleshooting Common Problems

When results don't match expectations, systematic diagnosis identifies correctable issues.

Problem: Posting consistently but engagement is low. Diagnosis: Content may not resonate with your audience, posting times may miss peak activity, or hooks may fail to stop scrolling. Solution: Analyze which posts get any engagement versus none. Identify patterns. Test different content types, formats, and posting times systematically.

Problem: Engagement is fine but no business results. Diagnosis: Audience may not match target market, content may not show relevance to business offering, or conversion path may have friction. Solution: Analyze follower demographics against customer demographics. Audit content for business relevance. Test different calls to action and landing pages.

Problem: Growth plateaued despite consistent effort. Diagnosis: May have saturated accessible audience, content may have become stale, or strategy may need evolution. Solution: Test adjacent topic expansion. Introduce new content formats. Consider partnerships or paid amplification to reach new audiences.

Problem: Can't maintain consistent posting. Diagnosis: Cadence may exceed sustainable capacity, batching system may have failed, or X priority may be too low relative to other demands. Solution: Reduce posting frequency to sustainable level. Rebuild batching habit. Reassess whether X warrants the time investment given other priorities.

Success Metrics by Business Type

Different businesses should weight different metrics based on their goals.

Service businesses: Weight lead generation metrics heavily. Track inquiry volume, inquiry quality, and conversion from inquiry to client. Follower growth matters only if it correlates with inquiry growth.

E-commerce: Weight traffic and conversion metrics heavily. Track click-through to site, add-to-cart from X traffic, and purchases attributed to X. Engagement metrics matter only if they correlate with sales.

Content creators: Weight audience growth and engagement metrics heavily. Track follower growth rate, engagement rate trends, and content consumption metrics. Monetization metrics matter as revenue streams develop.

Personal brands: Weight visibility and authority metrics. Track mentions, shares, and inbound opportunities (speaking invitations, media requests, collaboration proposals). The goal: often reputation more than direct revenue.

Nonprofits: Weight awareness and action metrics. Track reach, engagement with mission content, and conversion to desired actions (donations, volunteer signups, advocacy participation).

Match your measurement emphasis to your actual goals. Generic metric priorities from other contexts may not serve your specific situation.

ADDITIONAL CASE STUDIES AND PRACTICAL EXAMPLES

Extended Case Study: From Zero to Authority

This detailed case study illustrates the complete journey from new account to established authority, showing how the principles throughout this book combine in practice.

Starting Point: A management consultant specialized in operational efficiency for mid-sized manufacturing companies. Despite fifteen years of industry experience and strong referral business, her X account had 127 followers accumulated over three years of sporadic posting. She had posted 34 times total, mostly reshares of industry news without commentary. No clear positioning. No engagement strategy. No measurable business impact.

Month One: Foundation Building. She completed profile optimization in a single three-hour session. New header image featuring her tagline "Operational Excellence for Manufacturing" with three client logos showing social proof. Bio rewritten to "Manufacturing ops consultant | Helping mid-size manufacturers cut waste 30%+ | 15 years, 60+ plants optimized | Free assessment: yoursite.com/assess." She pinned a thread explaining her assessment methodology. She defined three content pillars: Operational Best Practices at 40 percent, Client Transformation Stories at 35 percent, and Industry Trends at 25 percent.

Month Two: Content and Engagement Launch. She conducted her first monthly batching session, generating 24 posts across pillars. She posted four times weekly on consistent schedule. She began engaging with manufacturing industry conversations, adding thoughtful replies to discussions about supply chain challenges, workforce issues, and efficiency techniques. She spent 30 minutes daily on engagement in addition to posting.

Month Three: Pattern Recognition. Analytics revealed that case study content dramatically outperformed other pillars on engagement metrics. Posts showing specific waste reduction percentages generated three times the engagement of general best practice tips. She adjusted pillar allocation to emphasize transformation stories more heavily.

Months Four through Six: Acceleration. She collaborated with a manufacturing software company whose audience overlapped with hers, co-authoring a thread series about technology-enabled efficiency improvements. The partnership introduced her to 4,000 new potential followers. She began receiving direct messages asking about her services, three to four weekly compared to zero previously.

Twelve-Month Targets: meaningful follower growth, though vanity metrics matter less than business outcomes. The real goals: qualified inquiries from decision-makers at target companies who initiate contact after following content, with some converting to consulting engagements. Documented parallel: Trade Press Services confirms X algorithms favor consistent presence for B2B reach development. Her industry reputation shifted from good consultant if you know her to thought leader in manufacturing operations. Research from Trade Press Services confirms this pattern: X algorithms favor consistent presence, enabling pipeline development that transforms industry positioning over time.

Key factors in her success: Completing foundation work before launching content. Consistent posting maintained through batching systems. Active engagement beyond just publishing. Data-driven content adjustment based on performance. Strategic partnership expanding reach. Patient persistence through slow early months. Rigorous attribution tracking proving business value.

Extended Case Study: Nonprofit Audience Transformation

This case study shows how intentional audience quality focus outperforms pure growth optimization.

Starting Point: A regional food bank with 8,400 followers accumulated over five years of inconsistent posting. High follower count masked low quality: most followers came from a viral moment three years prior, attracting entertainment-seekers rather than potential donors or volunteers. Engagement rate was 0.3 percent, well below the 1 percent minimum indicating audience health.

The Problem Diagnosis: Analysis revealed that most followers had no connection to the food bank's mission or service area. They had followed for contest entries, entertaining content, or trending topic participation unrelated to hunger relief. When the food bank posted about its actual work, these followers ignored it or unfollowed. The audience was large but wrong.

The Strategic Shift: Rather than continuing growth tactics, leadership approved focus shift to audience quality over quantity. Staff accepted that follower count would likely decline during transition.

New Content Strategy: Every post connected directly to mission. Impact stories showing families served. Volunteer spotlights showing community involvement. Food insecurity statistics for the service region. Donation impact explanations showing exactly what contributions accomplished. Behind-the-scenes looks at operations. No more contests. No more trending topic chasing. No more content unrelated to hunger relief.

Six-Month Results: Follower count declined from 8,400 to 6,100 as entertainment-seeking followers unfollowed. But engagement rate climbed from 0.3 percent to 2.1 percent as remaining audience proved genuinely interested in the mission. The smaller, engaged audience outperformed the larger disengaged one: $42,000 in donations came directly from X traffic during the measurement period. Charity:water showed similar dynamics at scale, raising $250,000 in 48 hours through their Twestival campaign by focusing on mission-aligned engagement over follower count.

Twelve-Month Results: Follower count recovered to 7,800 through organic growth of mission-aligned followers. Engagement rate stabilized at 1.8 percent. Donation attribution reached $42,000 annually. Major donor cultivation began through X relationship building, with two significant gifts totaling $75,000 partially attributed to X engagement.

Key lessons: Audience quality determines value more than audience size. Growth tactics attracting wrong audience waste resources and damage results. Intentional audience building around mission creates sustainable engagement. Short-term follower decline can enable long-term value growth. Mission-focused content attracts mission-aligned audience.

Platform-Specific Writing Guide

Writing effectively for X requires understanding how the platform's constraints shape communication.

Character Limits and Their Implications: Free accounts have 280 character limit per post. Premium accounts extend to 25,000 characters. But longer isn't always better. Data consistently shows that shorter posts receive higher engagement rates on average. The constraint forces clarity. Write what matters. Cut what doesn't.

Effective Post Structure: Front-load the most important information. X users scroll quickly. If your key point appears in sentence three, many readers will never reach it. Put your hook first.

Put your main insight early. Put supporting details and caveats later.

Thread-Specific Writing: Each tweet in a thread must work independently while contributing to the whole. Number your tweets to orient readers. Include clear transitions. Make the first tweet compelling enough to earn continued reading. Make the final tweet summarize and prompt action.

Voice Consistency: Your X voice should be consistent across posts while appropriate to the medium. X rewards conversational tone more than formal business writing. X rewards opinions and perspectives more than neutral information delivery. Find your authentic voice and maintain it consistently.

Calls to Action: Every post should have purpose, but not every post needs explicit CTA. Content-focused posts build trust and engagement. Occasional conversion-focused posts use that trust. Balance matters: too many CTAs fatigues audience, too few wastes accumulated attention.

Engagement Tactics Reference

Quick reference for engagement strategies covered throughout the book.

Reply Strategy: Add value, don't just agree. Reference specific points from the original. Keep replies focused and concise. Time replies to high-profile posts for maximum visibility.

Quote Post Strategy: Add your perspective on why content matters. Provide context the original lacks. Disagree respectfully with reasoning. Connect to your expertise.

Conversation Starters: Ask specific, answerable questions. Share opinions inviting debate. Request additions to lists or ideas. Acknowledge others' expertise.

Community Participation: Find your niche communities and participate consistently. Add value in conversations beyond your own posts. Build relationships through genuine engagement over time.

Follow and Engagement Patterns: Follow accounts whose content you actually want to see. Engage consistently with accounts you want to build relationships with. Unfollow accounts that no longer serve your interests.

Content Format Reference

Quick reference for content formats covered throughout the book.

Text Posts: Fastest to create. Best for quick insights, opinions, and engagement prompts. Keep tight and focused.

Threads: Best for complex ideas, frameworks, and stories. Structure each tweet to stand alone. Use for content that needs more depth than single post but doesn't warrant separate article.

Images: Best for data visualization, screenshots proving claims, behind-the-scenes moments. Use PNG for graphics, JPEG for photos.

Video: Best for demonstrations, personal connection, complex explanations. Keep under 60 seconds for highest completion. Prioritize audio quality.

Polls: Best for engagement and audience research. Keep choices clear and limited. Use results to inform content strategy.

Measurement Quick Reference

Key metrics and targets covered throughout the book.

Engagement Rate: Likes plus replies plus reposts divided by impressions. Target 1 to 3 percent for accounts under 10,000 followers. Expect decline as audience grows.

Engagement Quality Ratio: Replies plus quotes plus link clicks divided by total engagements. Target 0.25 to 0.40 indicating active rather than passive audience.

Follower Growth Rate: New followers per week. Target 5 to 20 for accounts under 1,000. Target 50 to 200 for accounts 1,000 to 10,000.

Profile Conversion Rate: New followers divided by profile visits. Establish your baseline before optimization, then track improvement. Higher rates indicate more effective profile elements.

Link Click-Through Rate: Clicks divided by impressions on link posts. Target 2 to 5 percent for valuable destinations.

Attribution Coverage: Tracked links divided by total links. Target 95 percent to ensure meaningful attribution data.

Tool Quick Reference

Categories of tools mentioned throughout the book.

Scheduling: Buffer, SocialBee, Hootsuite, Later. Choose based on platform count, team size, and budget.

Analytics: Native X Analytics (Premium required for full access), third-party dashboards for cross-platform reporting.

Graphics: Canva for templates and simple design, stock photo sites for imagery.

Video: Native phone camera for authenticity, Loom for screen recording, basic editing apps for cleanup.

Link Management: Bitly or Rebrandly for shortened links with UTM parameters and click tracking.

Monitoring: Google Alerts for mentions, social listening tools for comprehensive monitoring.

COMPREHENSIVE INDUSTRY APPLICATIONS

X Strategy for Professional Services

Professional services firms face unique X challenges and opportunities that merit specific guidance.

The trust requirement is paramount. Clients hiring consultants, accountants, attorneys, or other professional services make high-stakes decisions based on expertise and trust. X content must establish both. Showing expertise through substantive insights matters more than volume. Showing judgment through thoughtful analysis matters more than showing knowledge through information sharing.

Content themes that work for professional services: Case studies showing specific client results build credibility through evidence. Frameworks and methodologies show systematic thinking clients want to hire. Industry analysis shows you understand the context clients operate in. Common mistake identification shows you know what to avoid. Process explanations show what working with you looks like.

Content themes to avoid: Generic business advice everyone knows. Self-promotional content without value delivery. Controversial political opinions that alienate potential clients. Complaints about clients or industry frustrations.

Engagement strategy for professional services: Position yourself in conversations where potential clients observe. Add substantive commentary to discussions in your specialty area. Build relationships with referral sources and complementary service providers. Avoid engaging in arguments or controversial debates that could concern potential clients.

Lead generation for professional services: X builds awareness and credibility that generates inbound inquiries. Free assessments, audits, or strategy sessions offered through pinned posts convert engaged followers to conversations. Follow-up systems convert conversations to engagements.

X Strategy for E-Commerce

E-commerce brands face different X dynamics than service businesses.

Product showcase content must balance promotion with value. Constant product posts without variety exhausts audience attention. Interweave product content with customer stories, behind-the-scenes glimpses, and lifestyle content showing products in use.

User-generated content provides social proof more authentic than brand content. Encourage customers to share their purchases and experiences. Reshare and acknowledge customer content to encourage more. Build community around product usage and brand identity.

Customer service on X is often expected for e-commerce brands. Monitor mentions and respond quickly to issues. Public resolution of problems shows responsiveness. Private channels for complex issues protect customer privacy while showing you care.

Promotional timing requires strategy. Launch announcements, sales, and limited offers can drive traffic and conversion. But constant promotional content depletes audience goodwill. Balance promotional content with value content at roughly 20 percent promotional, 80 percent value.

Influencer and partnership opportunities are extensive for e-commerce. Product gifting to relevant creators expands reach. Affiliate relationships create aligned incentives. Collaborative content with complementary brands reaches new audiences.

X Strategy for Creators and Media

Creators building audience and monetizing attention face X-specific opportunities.

Content serialization builds habit and anticipation. Regular features that audiences expect and anticipate create engagement patterns. Weekly series, recurring themes, and predictable content types help audiences know what to expect and return for.

Personality-forward content uses the creator's unique voice and perspective. Unlike brands that must maintain professional distance, creators can share opinions, reactions, and personal moments that build connection. Authenticity and consistency matter more than polish.

Multi-platform strategy uses X as part of broader ecosystem. X often serves as discovery and engagement layer driving traffic to longer-form content on YouTube, podcasts, Substack, or other platforms where deeper monetization happens.

Community building creates superfans who support monetization. Engaged communities justify premium offerings, memberships, and exclusive content. X enables direct relationship with audience that supports premium positioning.

Direct monetization through Creator Revenue Sharing provides baseline income for qualifying accounts. But indirect monetization through sponsorships, products, services, and premium content typically exceeds direct platform payments significantly.

X Strategy for Nonprofits

Nonprofits face resource constraints and mission requirements that shape X strategy.

Mission alignment must guide all content. Unlike businesses that can experiment broadly, nonprofits must show consistent focus on their charitable purpose. Content unrelated to mission raises questions about organizational focus and appropriate use of resources.

Story-driven content humanizes abstract causes. Statistics inform but stories move. Beneficiary stories with appropriate consent, volunteer spotlights, and impact narratives create emotional connection that statistics alone can't achieve.

Donor cultivation happens through engagement over time. Major donors often follow and observe organizations before making significant commitments. X provides window into organizational values, competence, and impact that influences giving decisions.

Volunteer recruitment benefits from behind-the-scenes content showing what volunteering involves. Clear calls to action for volunteer opportunities convert interested followers to active participants.

Advocacy and awareness for causes can expand beyond existing supporter base. Strategic use of relevant hashtags, engagement in policy discussions, and partnerships with aligned organizations extend reach to potential supporters who share values but don't yet know the organization.

Seasonal and Cyclical Content Planning

Many businesses experience seasonal patterns that should inform X strategy.

Anticipate and prepare for peak seasons. If your business has busy seasons, create content in advance during slower periods. Bank content for times when you will be too busy to create. Schedule seasonal promotions and campaigns ahead.

Capitalize on industry events and calendar moments. Industry conferences, trade shows, and professional events create conversation opportunities. Annual awareness days, holidays, and cultural moments relevant to your audience provide content hooks.

Adjust expectations for seasonal slowdowns. Many industries experience predictable slow periods. Engagement often declines during holidays and summer months for B2B content. Maintain minimum presence but don't expect peak performance during known slow periods.

Plan content themes across annual calendar. Map your content pillars across the year considering seasonal relevance. Some themes work better at certain times. Planning enables alignment rather than reactive scrambling.

Platform Evolution and Adaptation

X continues evolving, requiring ongoing adaptation of strategy.

Feature changes require strategy updates. New features often receive algorithmic boost during rollout. Early adoption of new formats can provide visibility advantage. But not every new feature deserves adoption; evaluate fit with your goals.

Policy changes affect what content works. Platform policy evolves in response to regulatory pressure, competitive dynamics, and content moderation challenges. Stay informed through official announcements and adapt strategy accordingly.

Algorithm changes alter distribution patterns. Major algorithm updates can dramatically change what content receives distribution. Monitor your own metrics for unexpected changes. Adapt content approach based on what the algorithm currently rewards.

Competitive dynamics shift over time. New platforms emerge. Existing platforms evolve. Your competitors change their strategies. Continuous learning and adaptation enables sustained success despite changing conditions.

The consistent principles matter more than specific tactics. Providing value to your audience, building genuine relationships, measuring what matters, and adapting based on evidence remain constant even as platform specifics change.

Long-Term Success Principles

Across all the tactical guidance in this book, certain principles enable sustained success.

Patience over urgency. X success builds over months and years, not days and weeks. Quick fixes rarely last. Sustainable approaches compound over time. Accept slow early progress as investment in eventual acceleration.

Quality over quantity. One excellent post outperforms five mediocre posts. One genuine relationship outperforms twenty superficial connections. One qualified lead outperforms fifty unqualified followers. Prioritize depth over breadth.

Consistency over intensity. Showing up reliably at sustainable pace outperforms heroic bursts followed by exhausted silence. Build systems enabling consistency. Protect sustainable practice.

Authenticity over optimization. Your genuine voice and perspective differentiate you. Optimizing toward generic best practices produces generic results. Bring your actual expertise and real personality.

Business outcomes over vanity metrics. Followers and likes feel good but don't pay bills. Focus measurement and optimization on metrics that connect to actual business results.

Relationships over transactions. X rewards accounts that participate in community rather than just broadcast. Build relationships. Add value to others. Create reciprocity through generosity.

Learning over perfection. Every post teaches something. Every campaign provides data. Continuous improvement based on evidence beats waiting for perfect strategy. Start, measure, learn, improve.

These principles transcend specific tactics and platform features. They enable adaptation as circumstances change while maintaining focus on what actually drives results.

Your X journey begins with first post after closing this book. What you do consistently over the next six months matters more than any specific tactic you learned in these pages. Begin. Persist. Measure. Improve. The results will follow.

ADVANCED STRATEGY CONSIDERATIONS

Building a Content System That Scales

As your X presence grows, the approaches that worked at 500 followers may not scale to 5,000 or 50,000. Understanding how to evolve your systems enables sustained growth without proportional increase in time investment.

Content repurposing extends the value of your best work. High-performing threads can become blog posts reaching different audiences. Blog posts can become thread series reaching X audiences. Key insights can become recurring content touchpoints. One piece of strategic thinking generates multiple content pieces across formats.

Engagement systems must scale beyond personal management. At smaller scale, you can personally respond to every reply and mention. At larger scale, this becomes impossible. Decide what engagement requires your personal attention versus what can be handled by team members or deprioritized. Protect time for high-value engagement while accepting you can't respond to everything.

Content production can involve support without losing authenticity. Researchers can gather data and sources you then synthesize. Editors can refine your drafts while preserving your voice. Schedulers can handle logistics while you focus on creation. The core strategic thinking and authentic voice must remain yours, but support functions can scale capacity.

Measurement complexity increases with scale. Larger audiences generate more data requiring more sophisticated analysis. Attribution becomes more important as business stakes increase. Consider investing in better tools and potentially dedicated analytics support as scale justifies the investment.

Managing Multiple Account Types

Some organizations manage multiple X accounts serving different purposes. Understanding how to coordinate multiple accounts prevents confusion and conflict.

Brand versus personal accounts: Many professionals maintain both company account and personal professional account. These serve different purposes. Brand accounts represent organizational voice. Personal accounts represent individual perspective. Content should differ appropriately. Cross-promotion should feel natural rather than forced.

Product versus company accounts: Companies with multiple products sometimes maintain separate accounts. This works when products have distinct audiences. It creates overhead when audiences overlap significantly. Evaluate whether account separation serves audience needs or just internal organizational structure.

Regional versus global accounts: International organizations sometimes maintain region-specific accounts, enabling local relevance but creates coordination challenges. Ensure consistent brand voice across accounts while allowing appropriate local adaptation.

Coordination requirements: Multiple accounts require clear ownership, content calendars, and approval processes to prevent conflicts. Who can post what to which account? How do accounts reference each other? What happens when accounts could both address the same topic?

Crisis Prevention and Reputation Protection

Beyond crisis response covered in Chapter 15, proactive reputation protection reduces crisis likelihood.

Content review processes catch problems before publication. Even quick review by a second person catches issues the creator missed. For sensitive topics, formal approval processes may be appropriate.

Media training prepares for interview and public speaking situations where missteps could generate negative X attention. Understanding how statements might be quoted, screenshotted, or taken out of context informs more careful communication.

Monitoring enables early detection of emerging issues. Social listening tools, Google Alerts, and regular search of brand mentions surface potential problems before they escalate. Early intervention often prevents full crisis development.

Relationship building creates goodwill that provides buffer during difficulties. Organizations with strong community relationships receive benefit of the doubt during ambiguous situations. Goodwill accumulated through consistent positive engagement becomes asset during challenging moments.

Documentation protects against false claims. Records of what was actually said, when, and in what context enable factual response to inaccurate characterizations. Screenshot your own posts. Archive important conversations. Maintain records enabling accurate history.

Competitive Intelligence and Differentiation

Understanding your competitive environment on X informs strategy and enables differentiation.

Competitor monitoring reveals what others in your space are doing. What content themes dominate? What seems to perform well? Where are gaps you could fill? Regular review of competitor accounts provides strategic intelligence.

Differentiation through approach rather than just topics helps you stand out. Many accounts may discuss similar topics. How you discuss them, what perspective you bring, and what voice you use differentiates. The same topic covered in your unique way becomes distinct from competitors covering it their way.

Gap identification through competitor analysis reveals opportunities. What questions does your audience have that competitors don't address? What perspectives are missing from industry conversation? What value could you uniquely provide?

Benchmark appropriate comparison accounts carefully. Compare your performance against accounts at similar stage and in similar niche. Comparing yourself to accounts with dramatically different resources, audiences, or tenure provides misleading benchmarks.

International and Multilingual Considerations

Accounts serving international audiences face additional complexity.

Language decisions affect reach and engagement. Posting primarily in English reaches largest potential audience but may limit engagement from non-English speakers. Posting in multiple languages requires additional content creation capacity. Single-language accounts may better serve specific markets deeply than multi-language accounts serve multiple markets shallowly.

Cultural adaptation extends beyond translation. Humor, references, and communication styles vary across cultures. Content that resonates in one market may confuse or offend in another. Cultural consultation improves content for international audiences.

Time zone management enables global reach. Posting at consistent local time reaches different time zones at different local times. Consider posting the same content multiple times to reach different geographic audiences at appropriate local times.

Regional variations in platform usage affect strategy. X's relative importance varies by market. User behavior and expectations vary by region. Strategy that works in one market may not translate directly to others.

Building Your Personal Advisory Network

X strategy benefits from outside perspective beyond self-analysis.

Peer networks provide mutual support and shared learning. Finding others at similar stage pursuing similar goals enables sharing what works, what doesn't, and mutual encouragement through challenges.

Mentors with X success in your space can provide guidance informed by relevant experience. Identify potential mentors through observing who succeeds with similar audiences and approaches.

Accountability partners help maintain consistency. Committing to report your posting consistency to someone else creates external motivation supplementing internal discipline.

Professional communities organized around X strategy and social media marketing provide ongoing education and connection. Industry conferences, online communities, and professional associations offer learning and networking opportunities.

Consultants and coaches provide expert guidance for accounts willing to invest in accelerated learning. The right coach matches your needs, stage, and goals. Evaluate carefully before engaging.

Your Next Steps

This book provides comprehensive framework for X success. But information without implementation produces no results. Here are your immediate next steps:

Today: Choose one action from this book and complete it. Profile optimization, content pillar definition, or analytics setup. Something concrete. Done today.

This week: Complete foundation work from Chapters 2 through 4. Optimized profile. Defined content pillars. Content bank with initial ideas. Baseline metrics documented.

This month: Launch consistent posting at sustainable cadence. First, batching session completed. Regular engagement begun. Tracking systems operational.

Next 90 days: Execute the 90-day implementation plan from Chapter 18. Build the habits that enable long-term success.

Ongoing: Return to relevant chapters as questions arise. This book serves as reference throughout your X journey, not just initial reading material.

The knowledge is now yours. The strategy is clear. What remains is execution.

Begin.

THE FACTICS METHODOLOGY SUMMARY

Throughout this book, you have encountered the Factics methodology woven into every chapter. This final summary consolidates the approach for quick reference and reinforcement.

The Three Elements

Facts establish reality through evidence. Every strategic recommendation in this book connects to documented data, platform statistics, or observed patterns. Facts prevent strategy based on wishful thinking or outdated assumptions.

Tactics translate facts into action. Knowing platform demographics means nothing without tactical application. Each fact in this book pairs with specific actions you can implement. Tactics without facts become guesswork. Facts without tactics become trivia.

Outcomes measure results. Every tactic connects to measurable goals enabling you to verify whether actions work for your specific situation. Without defined outcomes, you can't distinguish successful tactics from wasted effort. Outcomes close the loop from fact to tactic to result.

The Pattern in Practice

The pattern repeats throughout your X strategy:

Profile optimization: The fact that profiles convert 15 to 25 percent of visitors to followers when optimized leads to the tactic of completing all profile elements with strategic intent, measured by the outcome of tracking your actual conversion rate against this benchmark.

Content strategy: The fact that consistent posting drives three times faster follower growth leads to the tactic of establishing pillar-based content calendars with batching systems, measured by the outcome of calendar adherence rate and follower growth correlation.

Engagement approach: The fact that replies carry more algorithmic weight than likes leads to the tactic of creating content designed to spark conversation rather than passive approval, measured by the outcome of engagement quality ratio tracking reply percentage.

This pattern applies to every strategic decision. What does the evidence say? What action does that suggest? How will you measure whether it works?

Applying Factics Beyond This Book

The methodology extends beyond X strategy to any domain requiring evidence-based decision making.

When evaluating advice from any source, ask: What facts support this recommendation? What specific actions should I take? How would I measure whether it works?

When making strategic decisions, structure your thinking: What do I know about this situation based on evidence? What options does that suggest? How will I evaluate results?

When reviewing results, complete the loop: What actually happened? Does this match what facts predicted? Should I adjust tactics based on new evidence?

The Factics framework isn't just a book structure. It's a thinking discipline enabling better decisions across business and life.

Your Factics Implementation

Apply the methodology to your X strategy starting today:

Document your baseline facts. What does your current performance data show? What do you know about your audience from evidence rather than assumption?

Define specific tactics you will implement. What actions from this book will you take first? When specifically will you do them?

Establish measurable outcomes. What metrics will you track? What results would indicate success? What would prompt you to adjust approach?

Schedule reviews. When will you assess results against outcomes? Weekly tactical review? Monthly strategic review? Without scheduled review, measurement produces data but not learning.

The methodology works. The evidence from over two decades of refinement and countless implementations shows results. What remains is your application to your specific situation.

The facts are clear. The tactics are documented. The outcomes are defined. Implementation is now your responsibility.

Synthesis Across Contexts

A local coffee shop implemented the full framework over six months starting from 800 followers with no strategy. Profile optimization included behind-the-scenes header image showing roasting and clear bio identifying the specialty and location. Content pillars covered coffee education, community spotlights, and behind-the-scenes glimpses organized into four weekly posts. Engagement focused on local food community through genuine conversation. Measurement tracked follower growth and foot traffic correlation.

Targets: Meaningful follower growth over six months, measurable foot traffic improvement according to point of sale comparison, and trackable customer discovery attribution. Documented parallel: Coffee Groundz achieved 30 percent sales increase through similar engagement strategies. Investment was approximately four hours weekly.

The B2B SaaS CEO followed similar pattern in dramatically different context starting from 450 followers despite $2M product. Profile highlighted personal expertise rather than product features. Content focused on industry pain points his product addressed through frameworks and methodologies, never mentioning the product directly. Strategy: three posts weekly, founder voice, industry commentary.

Results: followers grew from 450 to 12,000 over eight months, $340,000 in pipeline attributed to X through rigorous source tracking, four enterprise deals closed from prospects who discovered him through the platform.

A nonprofit communications director applied the framework to mission advancement starting from 1,200 followers struggling to translate following into donations. Content emphasized impact stories and beneficiary outcomes rather than donation requests or organizational news. Engagement built community around shared commitment to the cause. Measurement tracked donations and volunteer signups attributed to X.

Targets: significant follower growth over ten to twelve months with quality improvement as mission-aligned audience replaces entertainment-seeking followers. Aim for meaningful crowdfunding attribution and volunteer signup growth. Documented parallel: Charity:water raised $250,000 in 48 hours through Twestival campaign coordination.

Different contexts, different specific tactics, same underlying pattern. Profile, content, engagement, measurement, iteration.

The Path Forward

X strategy isn't mysterious. The principles are clear in the pages you have read. The tactics are documented with specific guidance. What separates success from failure is implementation over time.

Start where you are with whatever resources and audience you currently have. There is no perfect time to begin, only continued delay that costs compound growth you could be building.

Use what you have rather than waiting for better tools, more time, or ideal circumstances. Constraints force creativity. Limited resources demand focus on what matters most.

Do what you can today rather than planning perfect campaigns for someday. Imperfect action beats perfect planning. One published post outperforms ten drafted posts waiting for final polish.

Consistency beats intensity. Showing up reliably over years outperforms heroic bursts followed by exhausted silence. Sustainable pace enables sustainable results.

Progress beats perfection. Each post teaches something. Each week of engagement builds relationships. Incremental improvement compounds into significant results over months and years that grand but abandoned plans never achieve.

Measure what matters and let data guide decisions. Abandon what doesn't work rather than hoping repetition will somehow change results. Double down on what does work to compound proven success.

Build relationships, not just audience. Engagement creates value that broadcasting can't. The accounts that thrive are the ones that participate in community rather than just publishing into it.

Play the long game. Sustainable growth compounds like interest. Quick fixes don't last and often damage longer-term potential.

The investment you make today pays dividends for years if you maintain it.

Begin.

DIGITAL FACTICS X

Quick Reference Guides

Quick Reference Guides

15 Quick Ways to Boost Engagement Without Extra Hours

These tactics derive from the research and case studies documented throughout this book. Each aligns with verified platform data and documented implementation results. Implement one per week and track your own results.

1. Reply to three posts in your niche before posting your own content each day. This warms up your engagement signals and puts you in front of relevant audiences before you ask them to engage with you. The algorithm rewards accounts that participate in conversations, not just broadcast.

2. Add a specific question to the end of your next five posts. Questions invite replies. Replies carry more algorithmic weight than likes. "What's your experience with this?" works better than hoping for comments.

3. Quote post instead of reposting. Adding your perspective takes 30 seconds and generates significantly more engagement than simple amplification because it shows thought and adds value.

4. Post your best content twice at different times. Your 9 AM post reaches different people than your 3 PM post. Repurposing strong content extends its reach without additional creation time.

5. Turn your best reply into a standalone post. When you write a thoughtful reply that generates engagement, that content deserves its own stage reaching your full audience.

6. Use numbers in your hooks. "3 mistakes killing your engagement" outperforms "Common engagement mistakes" because specificity creates curiosity and implies completeness.

7. Screenshot your results and post them. The algorithm prioritizes visual content that generates dwell time where users stop scrolling. Actual data from your analytics dashboard or customer testimonials as images builds credibility faster than text descriptions.

8. Ask your audience what they want. Poll them. Ask directly. "What topic should I cover next?" generates engagement while providing content direction for future posts.

9. Respond to every reply within two hours during your first 30 days. This trains both the algorithm and your audience that you're present and engaged, not just broadcasting.

10. Pin your best performing post. Your top content deserves the premium position every profile visitor sees first. Update monthly based on performance data from your analytics.

11. Add your take to trending topics in your expertise area. Timely relevance combined with domain expertise generates discovery from people searching trending terms. Always check what the trend is about before posting.

12. Thank people publicly for sharing your content. Recognition encourages more sharing and shows you're paying attention to your community.

13. Turn competitor weaknesses into your strengths. When you see complaints about competitors, create content addressing those exact problems your solution solves.

14. Post behind the scenes content showing your actual work. Authenticity generates connection that polished content can't replicate. Case studies show this content type consistently performs well.

15. End threads with explicit calls to action. "Repost if this helped" or "Reply with your experience" tells people what to do rather than hoping they figure it out.

X Hacks for Solopreneurs

Running a business alone means every minute counts. These tactics deliver maximum impact with minimum time investment.

The 20-minute daily system: Spend 10 minutes creating or scheduling content, 10 minutes engaging with others. This minimal viable presence maintains momentum without consuming your day. Protect this time like a client meeting.

Batch everything possible. Two hours monthly creating content beats 10 minutes daily scrambling. Create 20 posts in one focused session rather than starting from scratch each day.

Repurpose relentlessly. Your blog post becomes a thread. Your thread becomes individual posts. Your best posts become recurring content. One idea generates multiple content pieces.

Automate the mechanical. Scheduling tools handle publishing. Templates speed creation. Saved replies handle common questions. Reserve your creative energy for content that requires your unique perspective.

Track only metrics that matter for your business. For solopreneurs, this usually means: profile visits (are people finding you?), link clicks (are they taking action?), and inquiries (is this generating business?). Ignore vanity metrics that look good but don't pay bills.

Build systems before you need them. Create your content bank before it is empty. Schedule posts before you get busy. The time to build capacity is before crisis, not during.

Student Starter Pack for Profile Polish

Starting from zero requires different tactics than optimizing established accounts. This guide helps students and early-career professionals build their first effective X presence.

Your first profile optimization: Use a professional photo showing your face clearly. Write a bio stating what you study or do, what you care about, and what value you offer. Include your school or field if relevant to your goals.

Your first content strategy: Pick three topics you can speak to credibly based on your studies, projects, or interests. Post about these consistently rather than random thoughts about everything.

Your first engagement approach: Follow and engage with people doing what you want to do. Add thoughtful comments on their posts. Ask genuine questions. Build relationships with people slightly ahead of you, not just industry stars.

Your first 30 days: Post three times weekly minimum. Reply to five posts daily in your areas of interest. Track your follower growth and engagement rate weekly. Adjust based on what generates response.

Your first milestone: 500 followers achieved through consistent valuable content and genuine engagement, not follow-for-follow schemes. This foundation supports everything that follows.

Common student mistakes to avoid: Posting only about assignments or complaints. Using X like a personal diary rather than a professional tool. Following thousands hoping for follow-backs. Engaging with controversial topics that could damage future job prospects.

Time-Saving Toolkit

These tools save hours weekly when implemented correctly. Start with one, master it, then add others.

Scheduling tools save daily posting time. Buffer offers free tier handling basic needs. Native X scheduling works for simple workflows. More sophisticated tools like Hootsuite add features as needs grow. The right tool matches your posting volume and platform count.

Content capture tools prevent lost ideas. Apple Notes, Google Keep, or dedicated apps let you capture ideas instantly when inspiration strikes. Review captures during batching sessions. Never lose a good idea because you forgot it.

Analytics tools reveal what works. Native X Analytics with Premium provides essential data. Google Analytics tracks website traffic from X. UTM parameters enable attribution. Start simple, add sophistication as you learn what questions matter.

Design tools enable visual content without skills. Canva templates produce professional graphics quickly. Stock photo sites provide imagery. Screenshot tools capture results and testimonials. You don't need Adobe expertise for effective X visuals.

Writing assistance tools speed drafting. AI tools can generate starting points requiring human refinement. Grammar tools catch errors before posting. The edit button with Premium fixes mistakes within 1 hour of publication.

Time tracking reveals actual investment. How many hours weekly do you actually spend on X? Is return proportionate? Track for one month to establish baseline. Optimize based on data rather than assumptions.

Stories of Early Failures to Learn From

These documented failures from brands and businesses teach lessons that remain essential in 2026. Each story shows why human judgment and governance matter more than automation and speed.

The Automated Empathy Disaster

During activist protests in 2013, activists tweeted grievances at Bank of America. The bank's support team used an automated-sounding script to reply to every tweet, even those sharing personal hardship, with the exact same generic message: "We'd be happy to help you with this, please DM us."

The mistake: treating social media as a ticket-processing system rather than human conversation. They prioritized response time over context. X users punish robotic, context-blind replies. The lesson: never use copy-paste replies for sensitive topics. Read the room before engaging. Measure sentiment quality, not just response speed.

The Hashtag Hijacking Blunder

In 2014, DiGiorno Pizza's social team saw #WhyIStayed trending and immediately tweeted: "#WhyIStayed You had pizza." They did not check the tag's origin. It was a serious conversation about domestic violence survivors explaining why they stayed in abusive relationships.

The mistake: trend-jacking without due diligence. The team assumed a trend was a marketing opportunity without clicking to see the content first. Trending topics on X often originate from crisis or activism, not entertainment. The lesson: always read the Top and Latest timeline of a hashtag before joining. The goal: zero crisis apologies per year.

The Wrong Account Recovery

In 2011, a Red Cross social media employee accidentally tweeted from the official @RedCross account instead of her personal one: "Ryan found two more 4 bottle packs of Dogfish Head's Midas Touch beer... when we drink we do it right #gettngslizzerd."

The pivot that saved them: instead of firing the employee or issuing a stiff corporate denial, Red Cross humorously acknowledged it: "We've deleted the rogue tweet but rest assured the Red Cross is sober and we've confiscated the keys." Dogfish Head Beer joined in, urging fans to donate to Red Cross, turning a PR risk into a fundraising win.

The lesson: human errors happen. The reaction defines the outcome. Own mistakes immediately with humanity and humor when appropriate. Don't cover up. Pivot to community connection.

The Timing Catastrophe

On the day of the Casey Anthony "Not Guilty" murder verdict in 2011, #notguilty trended globally. Entenmann's tweeted: "Who's #notguilty about eating all the tasty treats they want?!"

The mistake: using a high-velocity legal news trend for lighthearted consumer marketing. X is a real-time news network first, a marketing platform second. The lesson: implement a news check protocol. If a legal verdict, disaster, or political event is trending, pause all clever or automated content. Target zero brand safety violations.

The Viral Overcommitment

A small bakery tweeted "Retweet this and get a free cookie!" expecting 50 retweets from locals. The tweet went viral with over 5,000 retweets. They did not have the inventory or budget to honor it, leading to angry customers arriving in-store expecting free cookies that did not exist.

The mistake: launching an open-ended offer on a platform with unlimited viral scale without terms and conditions. Virality is unpredictable. A small account can go global instantly. The lesson: always cap your offers. "First 20 people to RT" or "While supplies last" protects your business from success you can't fulfill.

How Governance Prevents These Failures

Each of these disasters could have been prevented by simple checkpoint-based governance. The HAIA-RECCLIN framework assigns specific roles that catch these errors before publication:

The Researcher role would have checked the hashtag origin before DiGiorno posted. The Liaison role would have recognized Bank of America's replies lacked appropriate context. The Navigator role would have flagged Entenmann's timing against breaking news. The Calculator role would have modeled the bakery's offer against viral scenarios.

Human judgment at key checkpoints prevents automation from creating crises. Speed without oversight creates disasters. Governance creates protection.

Structured Experimentation

Strategy should include structured experimentation. These low-stakes tests generate learning while building engagement. Document everything so your data beats generic advice.

The format experiment: For one month, alternate between text posts, images, videos, and threads. Track engagement by format. Visual content consistently outperforms text alone. Test whether these patterns hold for your specific audience.

The timing experiment: Post identical content at different times across two weeks. Monday morning versus Tuesday afternoon. Early versus late. Identify your audience's actual active windows rather than assuming industry averages apply. Your X Analytics reveals when your followers are online.

The hook experiment: Test different opening approaches on similar content. Curiosity gap versus direct value statement. Question versus assertion. Number-based hooks versus narrative openings. Track which hook styles generate engagement for your voice and audience.

The length experiment: Test short posts versus longer posts on similar topics. Some audiences prefer quick hits. Others engage more with detailed thinking. Find your audience's preference through data rather than assumption.

The engagement experiment: For one week, spend your engagement time only on replies. Next week, only on quote posts. Third week, only on original content. Compare results. The algorithm weights different engagement types differently. Optimize your time allocation based on what generates returns for your account.

Track these experiments systematically. Document what you tested, results observed, and lessons applied. This structured learning accelerates improvement faster than hoping random posting eventually works. Your 2026 strategy should be built on your own verified data, not generic advice that may not apply to your situation.

Appendix A: HAIA-RECCLIN Framework

Figure A.1: HAIA-RECCLIN Framework

This appendix provides detailed governance architecture for organizations requiring systematic AI oversight beyond the practical workflow guidance in Chapter 17.

Framework Overview

HAIA-RECCLIN, standing for Human Artificial Intelligence Assistant with seven operational roles, provides governance embedding checkpoints into content workflows. The framework prevents AI-related risks through distributed responsibility and clear human oversight rather than hoping individual vigilance catches all problems.

The seven roles distribute specific quality checks across AI-assisted content production:

Researcher handles source verification and claim documentation, ensuring factual accuracy through independent verification of AI-provided information.

Editor ensures voice alignment and factual accuracy in final outputs, maintaining consistent brand voice across all published content.

Coder manages prompt engineering and version control when using AI tools, optimizing AI outputs through refined prompting.

Calculator tracks provenance and metadata, documenting what was AI-generated versus human-created for transparency and auditing.

Liaison ensures disclosure compliance and legal requirements, managing any regulatory obligations around AI-generated content.

Ideator conducts sensitivity review and perception assessment, evaluating how content might be received by different audience segments.

Navigator provides final approval and accountability, making publication decisions with full awareness of AI involvement.

Application to X Strategy

For X content production specifically, the framework operates through phases:

Research phase: AI assists gathering data, finding sources, and organizing information. Human researcher verifies accuracy and relevance of AI-found materials before use.

Drafting phase: AI generates initial content options based on verified research. Human editor selects among options, revises for voice, and refines for quality.

Review phase: Human reviewer checks voice consistency ensuring content sounds like you, factual accuracy catching any remaining errors, and policy compliance avoiding platform violations.

Publication phase: Human navigator makes final approval decision. AI may handle scheduling mechanics after approval.

Analysis phase: AI assists pattern recognition in performance data. Human interprets implications and decides strategic adjustments based on AI-surfaced insights.

Implementation Principles

Human judgment remains sovereign over all consequential decisions. AI provides capability amplification helping humans work faster and see more, not authority delegation where AI makes decisions autonomously.

Documentation enables accountability. Track what AI generated, what humans modified, and who approved each piece of published content. This documentation supports auditing and improvement.

Transparency builds trust with audiences. Disclose AI assistance when relevant to audience expectations and when disclosure requirements apply.

Verification prevents errors. AI outputs require human fact-checking regardless of how confident the AI sounds. Never assume AI-provided information is accurate without independent verification.

Appendix B: Sources and Further Reading

Appendix B: Sources and Further Reading

All sources referenced throughout this book are compiled here for reference. Platform documentation was accessed between September and November 2025. Statistics and research findings reflect data available at time of writing. Readers should verify current platform features and policies through official X documentation at help.x.com as the platform evolves rapidly.

Platform Statistics and Research

Buffer. (2014). The ideal length of everything online, backed by research. https://buffer.com/resources/the-ideal-length-of-everything-online-backed-by-research

Buffer. (2018). Foster Coffee Company case study: How a local coffee shop grew to 15,000 followers. https://buffer.com/resources/foster-coffee-company-case-study

Bullas, J. (2025). Social media statistics and research. https://www.jeffbullas.com/social-media-statistics

Business of Apps. (2025). X (Twitter) revenue and usage statistics. https://www.businessofapps.com/data/twitter-statistics

DemandSage. (2025). X (Twitter) statistics: Users, revenue, and key metrics. https://www.demandsage.com/twitter-statistics

Epic Owl. (2025). Video engagement research on X. https://epicowl.com/video-engagement-research

Exploding Topics. (2025). X (formerly Twitter) user age, gender, and demographic stats. https://explodingtopics.com/blog/x-user-stats

Hootsuite. (2025). How to schedule X posts: The complete guide. https://blog.hootsuite.com/how-to-schedule-tweets

Inspire to Thrive. (2025). X Premium features and edit button guide. https://inspiretothrive.com/twitter-premium-features

Miss Techy. (2025). X platform statistics. https://misstechy.com/x-platform-statistics

Sprout Social. (2025). X/Twitter statistics marketers need to know. https://sproutsocial.com/insights/twitter-statistics

Statista. (2025). Number of X (Twitter) users worldwide. https://www.statista.com/statistics/303681/twitter-users-worldwide

StatsUp. (2025). X engagement benchmarks.https://statsup.io/x-engagement-benchmarks

X Business. (2025). Video on X. Creative ad specifications. X Ads campaigns 101. https://business.x.com

X Help Center. (2025). About X Premium. About X Analytics. Creator revenue sharing eligibility. https://help.x.com

WebFX. (2025). How much does X advertising cost? https://www.webfx.com/social-media/pricing/twitter-advertising-cost

Academic Research

Rauschnabel, P. A., Sheldon, P., and Herzfeldt, E. (2019). What motivates users to hashtag on social media? Psychology and Marketing, 36(5), 473-488. https://doi.org/10.1002/mar.21191

Case Study Sources

Buzz Radar. (2023). Social media fails: Lessons learned from big brands. https://buzzradar.com/social-media-fails

Campaign Creators. (2017). Big brand tweet fails. https://campaigncreators.com/blog/big-brand-tweet-fails

CB Insights. (2017). Corporate social media fails. https://www.cbinsights.com/research/corporate-social-media-fails

Fit Small Business. (2025). Social media fails and contest failures. https://fitsmallbusiness.com/social-media-fails

Philosophy Communication. (2022). Epic Twitter blunders by big companies. https://philosophycommunication.com/twitter-blunders

Sendible. (2023). Common mistakes on Twitter to avoid. https://sendible.com/insights/common-twitter-mistakes

TopRank Marketing. (2023). Social fails and lessons. https://toprankmarketing.com/blog/social-fails-lessons

Success Case Studies

Avaya. (2012). Social media ROI case study: Enterprise B2B Twitter success. Documented in Social Media Examiner and industry presentations.

charity:water. (2009). Twestival global campaign results. https://www.charitywater.org

Welsh, J. (2024). Building a personal brand and creator business. https://www.justinwelsh.me

Additional Resources

For ongoing updates and supplementary materials, visit BasilPuglisi.com where chapter workbooks, templates, and current platform updates are available.

Thank you for reading. The strategies, frameworks, and tactics in these pages represent years of learning, testing, and refinement. They work when implemented with consistency and patience.

For downloadable templates, worksheets, and supplementary resources that extend the frameworks in this book, visit BasilPuglisi.com/resources. Your X success begins with the first action you take after closing this book. Make it today.

Copyright © 2025 by Basil C. Puglisi

Published by Digital Ethos

Second Edition: December 2025

For permissions requests or bulk purchase inquiries, contact: basilpuglisi.com

DIGITAL FACTICS X

BASIL C PUGLISI

www.ingramcontent.com/pod-product-compliance
Lightning Source LLC
LaVergne TN
LVHW052316200926
848481LV00002B/584